BREEDING WORKING DOGS

⊢ MICHAEL BRANDER

BREEDING
WORKING DOGS

MICHAEL BRANDER

Quiller

First published in the UK in 2008
by Quiller, an imprint of Quiller Publishing Ltd

British Library Cataloguing-in-Publication Data
A catalogue record for this book
is available from the British Library

ISBN 978 1 84689 003 1

Printed in Singapore by Stamford Press

Quiller

An imprint of Quiller Publishing Ltd

Wykey House, Wykey, Shrewsbury, SY4 1JA
Tel: 01939 261616 Fax: 01939 261606
E-mail: info@quillerbooks.com
Website: www.countrybooksdirect.com

CONTENTS

Historical development of canine breeding, both hunting and other varieties of dog. From pre-history to Roman times and in Britain from first different classification of breeds in sixteenth century by Dame Juliana Berners to development of breeding of specific hound types by various packs of hounds for over two hundred years before formation of the Kennel Club and modern database of different breeds. Different types of shepherding breeds, terriers, greyhounds, whippets and lurchers as well as gundogs developed. Gap between show and working specimens now wide.

Why breed? Have you thought it through? Long term commitment – time – costs – financial and other potential problems. Veterinary bills – suitable sire – fitness test honest assessment of bitch and sire for good and bad points – possible costs and advance preparations.

Seasons variable – six-monthly cycle normal – dog's reactions to bitch – spaying – exercise and kennelling arrangements – season pups born – difference between breeds – age when breeding – temperament – working versus non-working – town and country – show and working dogs – temperament differences – work differences – sporting Pekingese – mating teaser – showing colour – care of bitch in pup – signs of pregnancy.

waters burst – contractions – head of pup in mucous membrane – umbilical cord and afterbirth – drying pup – severing cord – antiseptic – squalling pup introduced to dam – allowed to suckle – next contractions – remove pup to box – leave last pup to suckle between contractions – allow bitch to move after two hours – Caesareans – whelpings usually at night – check over pups – deformed or injured pups best put down – differing attitudes to life and death – country and town – not in pup's best interests to try to save it if severely damaged – final clean up – check no afterbirth left – CCTV camera or window advantage – reaction of bitch varies – mild sedative possibly desirable.

Chapter 7 AFTER CARE OF BITCH AND PUPS | 125

Time spent with pups a matter of choice – modern technology useful – overlain pups and failure to suck – dew claws and tail docking - humane liberal attitude amongst vets – single dew claw missed can be troublesome – non-working versus working – pups best kept in semi-isolation while eyes closed – regurgitation by dam – feeding cholosterum hand rearing by bottle – after eyes open check reactions – more space required - introduction to milk feeding - call and whistle training start at once – developing personalities - outside refuge for bitch – fourth to fifth week introduce to mince balls – by sixth week regular feeding and begin weaning process - watching at play and feeding can assess individuals - check kennel ground daily for harmful debris – also possible dangerous pests – seventh to eighth week should be almost fully weaned and ready for new homes – look-alikes should be double-checked – KC documentation – tattooing and microchipping paper work – names should have been chosen and double checked with KC – details of injections and requirements for any being sent abroad – each country different – may mean keeping pup longer - costs borne by buyer – amateur and professional views - pitfalls of breeding versus satisfactions – long term view essential.

PREFACE AND ACKNOWLEDGEMENTS

One of the earlier readers of this book in typescript wanted 'cute' pictures of 'smiling' puppies, and accused me of 'insulting the reader's intelligence' by needless repetition. I am very well aware that at intervals throughout the various chapters I have stressed and repeated some points to the stage of possibly boring the reader, and occasionally this may seem tiresome, but there is a good reason for it. This is a book intended primarily for the absolute novice who wishes to breed from a bitch for the first time and knows absolutely nothing about it, possibly never having even owned a dog before. If I have at times seemed to get ahead of the game and later repeated similar points in another chapter this is because I want the novice reader to get into his or her mind as clear an overall picture of what to expect as possible.

This is not a straightforward matter. There is a great difference between breeding from small working dogs such as a Jack Russell and from larger breeds such as a Labrador or a lurcher. The former may have only one or two pups, whereas the latter may have ten or fifteen. The former may arrive on time and if it all goes well it may be over in half an hour or so with mother and pups thriving. The novice breeder may end up thinking it is all very simple and wondering what all the fuss was about.

It is very different dealing with ten or fifteen squirming little balls enclosed in bloody slimy membranes arriving at intervals of as much as two hours, sometimes wrongly positioned, with the dam occasionally straining convulsively and seemingly near to exhaustion. When some are near death on arrival and cannot appear to be revived the novice breeder will not have time to look up the relevant pages. Unless the warning signs are seen and noted and quick action taken a litter may easily be lost and sometimes the bitch as well, not only at such a time but also in the crucial weeks both before and after whelping. Breeding is not something to be undertaken lightly. There are certain points that are better repeated frequently at risk of boring the reader than overlooked at an important moment by the novice.

In a book of this nature on a subject such as this there are inevitably some areas where there is an element of repetition. When something may need doing on various occasions, but often in somewhat different ways or circumstances, this is difficult to avoid. For these reasons I make no apology for quite often repeating and emphasising points which I feel are of importance to the novice breeder and the bitch that might otherwise be overlooked.

Because this is intended as a guide for the novice breeder much of it will already be well known to anyone who has bred a number of litters. However, it is possible that even the experienced breeder may find a few useful tips and hopefully not too much to disagree with, although inevitably there are bound to be differing views on many aspects of breeding, as in most aspects of dog owning. I have done my best to indicate when there are different approaches to matters and indicated which in my view are preferable and why, but this is not intended to be an exhaustive textbook, merely a readable guide, and in this I hope it has been successful.

Breeding is anything but an exact science and everyone will have their own individual circumstances for which they will have to adopt their own solutions. Different breeds with different reactions and requirements, varied parts of the country, as well as a multiplicity of other personal circumstances, mean that every prospective breeder has to adapt to a range of diverse factors as well as his own bitch's behaviour and reactions. These may well vary considerably with each individual bitch. However, if this book does help anyone breeding for the first time from making any disastrous errors that in itself will have been worthwhile, and if it prevents any pups or even bitches from needlessly coming to harm, or possibly not even surviving, it will have been well worth writing.

For suggesting that I should write this book my thanks are due to my friend and editor, John Beaton, with whom I have worked closely on several other occasions over the years on widely diverse subjects. My grateful thanks are also due as usual to Evelyn, my long-suffering wife, who has been proofreading my books ever since I started writing. She also knows more about breeding and rearing puppies than most people and keeps me right on both matters. Finally, for vetting the manuscript I would like to thank my friend Neil Mollison MRCVS. For any errors or omissions, however, I am entirely to blame.

For the illustrations my grateful thanks must go to the following contributors: Tom Brechney, Jackie Drakeford, Jackie Gibbs, Colin Harrison, Carol Ann Johnson, Sue Rothwell and Michael Rufus.

Introduction | THE BACKGROUND

Originally dogs were all bred, consciously or unconsciously by humans for a distinct purpose – to gain food. Starting as animals hunting in a pack they were soon bred to hunt for man as the pack leader. Some were later bred not only for hunting but for protection, trained also to give warning of strangers approaching and to defend first the cave and later the home or settlement. Some were bred by nomadic tribes both as sentries and for war, trained to attack on command.

Inevitably, as mankind developed more settled living patterns so the role of dogs also changed. As a more settled agrarian society developed throughout the world, the role of the dog in society became stabilised, breeds of specialised animals began to be recognised and specific areas even became associated with certain particular types of dog. Some were used solely as guardians of the home and the livestock, while others were used solely for hunting.

As the methods of hunting changed, however, and became more sophisticated, so too did the roles of the dogs involved. While the hunting itself became more stylised, the different roles of the dogs when hunting steadily became more specialised. Some with powerful scenting abilities were developed as slow hounds, trained to search out and find the quarry when the scent was poor. Once the quarry was found and in full view, faster dogs, known as gaze hounds, trained to search by sight and pull down their quarry, were released. Once the quarry was held at bay the huntsmen moved in for the kill. The roles of both dogs and hunters had become steadily more specialised. Elderly and disabled animals, of course, at the end of their working lives may have graduated to become pensioners and so to pets.

By the time the rule of Rome had begun to spread from the Mediterranean area across Europe it is clear that hunting dogs had already developed very specific roles and the attitudes revealed in writings of that time were often surprisingly modern in tone. As far back as the first century AD the Roman writer Arrianus Flavius, anticipating the rules laid down by the National Coursing Club of Britain in 1858 by a substantial margin, wrote on hare coursing: 'The aim of the true sportsman with hounds is not to take the hare, but to engage her in a racing contest, or duel, and he is pleased if she happens to escape.' He was, of course, writing specifically of greyhounds, though referring to them under the generic term of 'hound'.

He went on to describe an imported Celtic greyhound and its relationship with him and his male partner in glowing terms which might almost have been written today, and showed a very laid-back attitude not always associated in most people's minds with a Rome where gladiatorial combat was regarded as a popular spectacle and animals and humans were regularly killed in the amphitheatre for the edification of the populace.

I once had a hound with the deepest possible blue-grey eyes, very quick, fond of work, full of spirit and sure of foot so that she could account for four hares in a day's sport. She is a most gentle creature (for I still have her with me as I write) and is most fond of company and I never knew a dog so devoted to me and my fellow huntsman, Megillus. When the day's run was over she never left him or me for a moment. She stays with me if I happen to be indoors. Comes alongside when I go out, follows me to the gymnasium, lies down when I am stripping, and on my way home goes in front, often looking back to make sure I have not taken some side turning – then finding all well she brightens and goes merrily on ahead again. If I have to go out on some city business she remains with Megillus and behaves in exactly the same way with him. If either of us happens to be ailing she never quits him. On seeing one or other of us after a short absence she jumps up gently in welcome and cries welcome too in the most friendly fashion. When we are at dinner she mouths one or other of us by the foot as a hint that she should have her portion. She has more language than any other dog I ever knew and can always tell you what she wants. If she has ever done wrong and if anyone uses the word *whip*, she goes to the speaker, crouches down begging, and puts her mouth up to be kissed; then jumping up with a grin she puts her paws on his shoulders, and will not release him until all signs of threatening temper have vanished. I should be quite willing to put the record of the name of my dog as a memorial, just as Xenophon of Athens had a dog remarkable for speed and cleverness and good manners which was also called Hermes.

Two young English Setters (Carol Ann Johnson)

This rather charming account of a Roman dog of possibly British breeding is among the earlier accounts of its kind. Such early records are rare, but it is clear that dogs must have been evolving alongside humans over the centuries. Throughout the world over the years distinctive types of dog had been bred and become recognised for their different roles and qualities. Surprisingly enough, however, the first British record of the different kinds of dogs in the country was written comparatively late, in 1486, by Dame Juliana Barnes or Berners, who wrote *The Boke of St Albans*. In it she noted, somewhat arbitrarily: 'This be the names of houndes. First there is a Grehown, a Bastard, a Mongrell, a Mastyfe, a Lemor, a Spanyell, Rachys, Kennetys, Teroures, Bocheris houndes, Myddyng dogges, Trindeltayles. And Prikherid curris. And smale ladies popis that beere a way the flees.'

Clearly there were already numerous different types of dog and many differing types of working dogs, as well as many that were bred purely as household pets or for more or less decorative purposes. Yet it was not until the mid nineteenth century that the Victorians with their love of rigid class distinctions began to distinguish between working and show strains of dogs and other animals. It is perhaps not always appreciated, however, that apart from fox and hare hunting, hare coursing was one of the earliest organised sports and the first where individual dogs competed against each other.

The earliest coursing club to be formed in Britain, the Swaffham Coursing Club, was founded by Lord Orford in 1766, but it was eclipsed in fame by the Altcar Club founded by Lord Sefton in 1825 on his estate near Liverpool, which became the centre for the sport. The Waterloo Cup, presented in 1836 by the owner of the Waterloo Hotel in Liverpool became the prize for a sixty-four dog stake in 1857, the equivalent to the Derby in horse racing. In 1858 a National Coursing Club was formed and established rules for the sport on the lines of the Jockey Club. Foremost amongst these rules it was laid down that a competitive trial between two dogs, and not the capture of the game, should be the aim. Presumably the committee formulating these rules was unaware that they had already been clearly stated by Arrianus Flavius in the first century BC, but it does show that even over the centuries the aims of true sportsmen remained the same. Killing for itself was never the aim and the game that escaped by its superior strength and skill was to be admired and applauded.

It was symptomatic of the Victorian era and its desire for organisation and classification in everything that the first Field Trials, for pointers and setters only, were held soon afterwards in 1865 at Southill in Bedfordshire on the estate of Mr S. M. Whitbread. The markings were forty for nose, thirty for pace and range, ten for temperament, ten for staunchness before and ten for staunchness behind. Trials for retrievers soon followed. Until then the only approach to trials had been wagers between sportsmen as to the number of birds that could be shot over their dogs, which tended to be more a match between the sportsmen themselves than their dogs.

Closer to a trial between individual working dogs at that period was the regular so-called sport in the Georgian and early Victorian era of releasing rats in a pit and wagering on the dog which killed the most rats within a given time. Like so many trials and wagers of the day, however, there were many fraudulent ways of influencing the results and as a consequence they gradually lost popularity and support. Popular in the more egalitarian Georgian era, they lost much support during the class conscious Victorian era, when they were seen as essentially 'lower class'. In much the same way shooting over pointers and setters gradually came to be regarded as no longer a 'gentleman's sport' by the nouveau riche Victorian sportsmen, whose aim was rather to shoot ever larger bags of reared and driven game with the newly invented double-barrelled ejector shotguns.

The first recorded dog show had meanwhile been held in Newcastle upon Tyne in 1859, and during the 1860s interest in shows increased very swiftly. By 1870 the various interests concerning dogs, particularly sporting dogs of various kinds, had become extremely diverse and often conflicting. Inevitably, with the typical Victorian desire to stratify society and organise separate and distinct classifications for everyone and everything, it was proposed in 1870 that a body be set up to legislate on all matters relating to dogs.

In 1873, as a result of this decision, the Kennel Club (KC) was founded as the premier body legislating on all canine matters. From this stage onwards, although it was a long time in becoming properly established, a national database of breeding was gradually developed. Pointers and setters and different breeds of retrievers were the first gundog groups to be included. Thereafter various different breeds were gradually recognised individually and their breeding first registered at the Kennel Club.

In 1878 Mr Charles Cruft, a dog biscuit salesman, organised the dog section of the Paris Exhibition, going on to organise similar annual canine exhibitions in the UK of dogs bred primarily for conformation and appearance rather than purely for their working ability. In 1938, on Mr Cruft's death, his widow asked the KC to take over the show with his name attached to it. What some have seen as the great divide between working dogs and conformation or show dogs of the same breeds had begun.

From the Kennel Club's formation in 1873, however, it was naturally a slow and very lengthy procedure to get the various breeds recognised and established. Once each was recognised and established as a separate breed their individual breeding had to be registered, quite apart from organising separate types of field trials with different rules for those requiring them, as well as recognising and recording all the different breed standards, in addition to organising the show side with approved judges for all the different competitions. It was a massive task and proved to be an extremely slow and still continuing process. Indeed spaniels, for instance, were not recognised until the first decade of the twentieth century, and the classification of the Hunt–Point–Retrieve (HPR) breeds occurred only in the 1950s. New breeds are still being steadily added. Lurchers and working terriers particularly, and quite a few collies and gundogs, are still bred quite widely on a haphazard basis by their owners, but the fact that a dog is officially unregistered and thus theoretically branded a mongrel does not by any means necessarily detract from its working abilities.

It is perhaps not widely appreciated that before the Kennel Club began to keep records of the various breeds very few canine pedigrees existed. Virtually the only breeding records that existed before then were those of

Bloodhound bitch and her puppy (Carol Ann Johnson)

various long established packs of foxhounds covering as much as two hundred years, or more in some cases. It is primarily because of this that huntsmen still refer to dogs other than hounds as 'cur dogs', or in effect mongrels.

Today there are many cross-bred labraniels, pointievers, spoodles and others which are the apple of their owner's eyes and are excellent working dogs. I am, however, by no means advocating breeding unregistered working dogs for, while a first cross may be excellent, too often the progeny of further crosses are a sad disappointment. Nevertheless, one has only to look at the multiplicity of what are generally termed 'cobs' in the horse world to appreciate that working abilities are not necessarily restricted to animals with a registered pedigree.

Before the advent of the Kennel Club, however, as noted, the only real documentation of breeding had been by some individual packs of foxhounds, and other types of hounds, going back a couple of hundred years or more in some cases. From this time onwards breeding was gradually recorded on a national level. Individual breeders have steadily been recorded so that a national database has been evolving over the years. The system relies to a large extent, of course, on the honesty of each breeder involved and there are ways in which it can be circumvented by unscrupulous individuals.

What in some quarters used to be referred to as 'behind the barn door matings' have sometimes been arranged by unscrupulous breeders for their own ends, for instance to ensure a suitable colouring in the offspring, or to bring in what was regarded by them as a desirable outcross. This can now, of course, be checked by means of DNA testing but it is virtually impossible to check every mating and there will probably always be people trying to beat the system for their own dishonest ends, just as there are bound to be judges who use their position to influence the results in favour of certain breeding lines. Unfortunately, although the Kennel Club does its best, it is difficult if not impossible to legislate against such infringements, which are exposed from time to time.

Dishonesty apart, careless breeding and failure to avoid inbreeding has unfortunately affected some breeds very adversely. This is apparently of little interest to some short-sighted individuals who continue with dangerously close inbreeding of stock that is already adversely affected by 'hysteria' or other endemic diseases. It is unfortunately also clear to see that in many working breeds the winning show lines are now utterly divergent from those winning in field trials or working tests, and they in turn are sometimes quite distinct from 'working' specimens. In some breeds it has even become tacitly, if not actually accepted, that the trends are so divergent that they can no longer be reconciled. This trend unfortunately shows little sign of altering and the divergence is very marked indeed in many breeds.

The situation regarding certain endemic diseases has become so bad in some breeds that they now require that any dog or bitch should be rated according to a strict set of rules in a bid to eradicate diseases which have become endemic due to careless inbreeding. Anyone wishing to breed must have their dog rated by a veterinary surgeon according to a regular scale for hip dysplasia and for cataracts, or incipient blindness. The costs of the hip test, which involves full anaesthesia and x-rays as well as manipulation, can be quite considerable, as can the ophthalmic test for cataracts and incipient blindness (PRA, Progressive Retinal Atrophy), which only a limited number of vets are licensed to conduct. The results for the hip tests are given promulgated on a scale in which the lowest readings are the most desirable and are given separately for right and left hand sides.

In that hopefully these measures may eventually eradicate these now endemic conditions in the breeds concerned this can only be welcomed but for those breeders involved it is another unwelcome but essential breeding cost. In due course, unless care is taken, other diseases such as entropion, or inturning eyelids, may have to be dealt with in a similar way, again mainly due to careless breeding. The Kennel Club is now well aware of such problems and is in the main ably supported by the breed societies concerned. Breeders have to abide by stringent Kennel Club and breed regulations if they wish to register their litters and in this way, hopefully, the situation will eventually be controlled. There will no doubt always be a small minority of unwitting breeders or rogues hoping to make a quick profit ignoring the system, but in the main, hopefully, these regulations should eventually succeed in their aim of eradicating such diseases from all the breeds concerned.

The whole art of breeding, however, is the ability to see where two animals complement each other and visualise how their progeny might improve on the sire and dam. In working breeds the knowledge of desirable conformation, together with how the body should work, and the importance of those sometimes difficult to define but all important qualities such as temperament, style, working ability, willingness to please, drive and determination, have to be weighed against the performances of sire and dam. To breed a perfect working combination that wins in the field and also wins in the show ring, excelling in the breed standards laid down, is extremely difficult and hence dual champions in field and show ring are rare indeed.

Although it may be the ultimate aim in the breeder's mind it is unlikely that both dog and bitch will ever complement each other perfectly. However, the ability to visualise in the mind's eye the progeny of a mating of two animals and to aim for perfection should be the ultimate long term goal of the serious breeder, whether for show or work. Regrettably, perhaps, it is probably easier to breed solely for conformation than for working ability, which may help to explain the steady divergence in type between show and working strains.

Another reason may well be that opportunities for working in the field in modern society are decreasing steadily with the ever increasing urbanisation of the countryside. For example many breeds of foxhounds that have taken centuries of selective breeding to reach their present standard of perfection may be lost due to the ban on fox hunting. Because this was imposed by people mostly unaware of the realities both of hunting and life in the countryside it could, however, never be completely successful. It is merely another example of how steadily increasing over-population in the limited

English Setter puppy feeding (Carol Ann Johnson) ————————————————————

space available in these islands has led to ever increasing divergence between town and country living.

As, however, Bernard Shaw is alleged to have said to the actress who proposed they should have a child on the grounds that with his brains and her physique it would be a world beater: 'Suppose, Madam, the child were unfortunate enough to have my legs and your brains ?' Therein, of course, is encapsulated the problem of any mating, but successfully visualising the progeny of any sire and dam and aiming for at least steady improvement should be possible. By thereafter breeding from the best of the litter it should be feasible to maintain steady improvement.

It will be appreciated, however, that this is not a short term aim. To bowdlerise Bernard Shaw, a chance one-night stand is unlikely to produce an Adonis, and in canine terms it is more likely to produce an unwanted mongrel. As in anything else, however, there are always the exceptions which prove, or disprove, the rule. Very little in life is certain and breeding any animals, but perhaps dogs especially, is always likely to be something of a gamble even with the apparently perfect sire and dam.

For any working breed of dog there are set breed standards which have been advocated as most suitable for that breed and its methods of working over the years by a committee of the senior members of the breed club. The old saying that a camel was a horse designed by a committee has unfortunately more than a kernel of truth. When that committee is constantly changing its membership over the years and amending the rules at intervals the horse is quite likely to end up with three humps, a giraffe neck and a trunk. This may be an exaggeration but there is a grain of truth in it, as anyone who has ever served on a committee, especially perhaps the committee of a dog club, will probably agree.

Every individual will have different views on what constitutes a perfect specimen of any given breed of dog regardless of the breed standards, or even within their limitations. It is up to each breeder, however, to try to keep as far as possible within those limitations while striving for his or her own ideas of perfection. Unfortunately it is here, almost immediately, that the abyss between breeders of show and working dogs begins to open.

While size and conformation may be measured accurately, there are other factors in any working dog which simply cannot be assessed in the same way. In all working dogs temperament above all else must be the most important factor. The desire to please, the readiness to obey, the understanding that their work in conjunction with their handler is the core of their being, these are amongst the most important features of any working dog. Without this basic temperament, without an inner calmness combined with drive and determination to work in conjunction with their handler, the working dog is incomplete. Yet this question of temperament encompasses a great deal and is very difficult to define accurately.

My first two foundation bitches were very unalike in temperament but each was outstanding in her own way. Both were extremely biddable and willing to please. One however was extremely intelligent and applied her mind to her work all the time. The other was full of instinct and could be relied on to use her nose and get results by that means above all. Working as a team together it was sometimes fascinating to watch them. With a wounded duck swimming downstream and occasionally diving, the one bitch would run along the bank keeping an eye on the proceedings ready at any moment to leap in and try to retrieve it herself if it seemed necessary, but otherwise content to watch her kennelmate following it down the river by scent, sometimes even diving underwater to retrieve it as she often would. It was a very interesting contrast in styles and temperament.

The highly intelligent bitch could mark a pricked bird fall two hundred yards away and retrieve it, even leaping in the air to catch it and return with it unharmed. The other could be set over a river to find a wounded bird that had fallen in thick gorse and would find the scent and follow the bird by scent and return with it alive. Each in her own way was outstanding and each knew the other's strengths and weaknesses and did her best to complement them, making them a remarkable team.

There was, for instance, a rounded hill where one or other would frequently point a rabbit near the top. The rabbit would bolt away round the hill through some gorse and sometimes, regrettably, was only wounded. It would then run round the hill to a small warren nearby where we were standing. The one would always follow it by scent and often find it if it was slowed down sufficiently. The other, after doing so once and seeing her quarry vanish down the hole near where it had started, always waited by the warren for the rabbit to arrive and then retrieved it before it could get down a hole, if the other had failed to retrieve it already. As a team they were complementary to each other and each in her own individual way was a very effective working dog. It might have been true that their working temperaments were very diverse, but they were each very successful in their very different ways and together were a memorable team to watch at work.

Just how much working ability can be equated with temperament, of course is difficult to define and the boundaries undoubtedly are often blurred as it plays such a large part in a working dog's make-up. In the gundog breeds there are other assets such as nose and softness of mouth, along with drive and willingness to please, which must be taken into account. In shepherding dogs the inbred understanding of how stock are likely to react, a natural affinity with their handler and a desire to excel. In greyhounds and lurchers the desire to follow by eye and chase, then swiftly kill. In terriers to kill at all costs and never to give in except to the will of their master. In all working dogs drive and determination to excel should be predominant, but always in conjunction with their handler. Yet let no-one forget that all dogs, though specially bred for generations, still have the same genes. I have seen terriers, lurchers, and collies which would both point and retrieve, and gundogs that would kill a rat or a fox, each of which would still perform what is generally regarded as their own roles without any transgressions.

Breeders should, however always try to avoid making any particular trait the be-all and end-all of their breeding. For instance, a soft mouth is often seen as the 'holy grail' for retrievers and it is indeed highly desirable in any retrieving dog, because mangled, uneatable game is no use to anyone. Nor should anyone ever try to justify any retriever which consistently breaks ribs or delivers game dead and badly mouthed. If the game is severely damaged then the retriever is simply not doing the job for which it was bred.

On the other hand I was present on one occasion while flighting duck when a spaniel came up to its owner in the darkness and clearly had something in its mouth it wished to deliver to him. He put his hand down confidently to accept the retrieve and immediately gave a yell of pain, which was followed by a brief struggle and a stream of curses. On enquiring as to the cause it appeared that the delivery to hand had proved to be a live rat that must have been attracted by the feed laid out for the duck. It had fastened onto his hand and, before he despatched it, gave him a particularly savage bite, for which he subsequently had to receive a series of painful injections against Weil's disease.

Quite how the dog had managed to carry the rat alive without being bitten itself is still something of a mystery. One has to assume it was carrying it by the scruff of the neck, like a puppy. Regardless of its carrying technique, although it was a very nice beast and an excellent working dog in the main, I personally do not rate that dog's intelligence very high even if it was very soft mouthed. It should have been able to distinguish instinctively between game and vermin.

I have known many very soft-mouthed retrievers that would still kill a rat without a moment's hesitation and obviously knew the difference between vermin and game very clearly. In a similar way many retrievers and other breeds of dogs, including one extremely fierce and unpredictable ex-police German Shepherd I have known, could retrieve an egg with its shell unbroken, but were extremely hard mouthed on a struggling bird or on a hare or rabbit, or in the case of the ex-police dog any struggling human being. Much depends in practice on their training and experiences as youngsters.

Hard mouth may very readily be caused by bad training, or by an unfortunate initial introduction to retrieving. For instance, allowing a young puppy to run in on wounded game and then kill it to stop it struggling may very easily result in a hard mouthed dog. It can almost certainly also be inherent, and caused by careless breeding from hard mouthed parents. When it comes to breeding it is better to be safe than sorry but hard mouth caused by careless handling is probably not inherent. It is, however, somewhat difficult for a prospective breeder to know whether the problem was caused by bad handling or bad breeding.

The gap between the breeder who aims at perfect conformation only and

Greyhound puppy feeding from her mother (Carol Ann Johnson)

the breeder who aims at the perfect working dog should not in theory be so very great. Dual champions in the gundog breeds, winning in both show ring and trials, though rare, are indeed still occasionally seen. Unfortunately the gap between good working dogs and good show types in most breeds is very wide indeed. There is also an unfortunate tendency for the breeders of working dogs to denigrate the show specimens and vice versa, which merely aggravates the problem and increases the divide between them. It has in many cases sadly reached the stage where the two are already completely irreconcilable.

It is also, unfortunately, only too common for owners and indeed breeders of some working breeds to refer contemptuously to other similar working breeds as if they were in some way inferior. In some cases this may stem from rivalry between breeds, which is understandable if still pathetic, but it can even extend on occasions to such petty matters as differences in colour within a single breed, which is totally absurd. Such attitudes are usually based on half baked misconceptions that have no sound basis in practice. To me they indicate a total lack of understanding and a completely blinkered mind, because anyone who likes dogs, and even those just beginning to learn about them, should appreciate good work by any breed of working dog, Any good working dog, working in complete affinity with its handler and performing well, should be a pleasure to watch regardless of its breed.

The sheepdog performing in perfect accord with its handler's whistles, signals or commands in moving a flock, or an individual sheep, the terrier quivering with eagerness at the entrance to the earth waiting for its master to give the command, or the greyhound just released, stretching every muscle and anticipating every movement of its quarry may all provide the knowledgeable spectator with a feeling of appreciation. Any gundog working well, finding game, steady to flush, shot and fall and then retrieving a difficult runner must be applauded by any unbiased knowledgeable spectator, regardless of the breed of dog. In the same way, a master of hounds working his pack to perfection as a single unit on the scent of a hare or fox is a joy to watch for the spectator who understands the perfect combination of man and hounds working together as a team.

A similar feeling of admiration may be had watching a first rate shot achieve a right and left at difficult wild birds, or a fisherman casting, hooking, playing and landing a hard fighting fish with suitable tackle, regardless of size, or come to that a stalker using the wind and ground to stalk and kill cleanly a deer. All are examples of successful interaction with animals in the wild, although in the cases above where the handler is acting in conjunction with a dog, or the hunter with his hounds, it is primarily the animals which are using their instincts in conjunction with the handler or huntsman. It is that willing collaboration and mutual understanding between the human and canine partners working in complete harmony which deservedly commands admiration.

The working dog is acting both in harmony and conjunction with its handler and interacting with other animals. Performed well this should always be worth watching and appreciating by any standards. Here is a case where human and dog working in complete accord are competing against the instincts, actions and reactions of another animal, or indeed animals, running free. To refuse to acknowledge the working abilities of any dogs other than those of the breed you own is truly inappropriate.

Whether the dog is working in a shepherding role, or as a hunting animal, and whether hunting by nose or by eye, the pleasure and indeed satisfaction to be had from any good piece of dog work should be almost as great for the spectator as for the handler. Even without a commentator to point out the finer pieces of dog work the average intelligent spectator can usually appreciate the almost magical accord between handler and dog to be seen at times during field or shepherding trials, or other occasions when people are working together with their dogs.

The intrinsic pleasure a working dog, or dogs, acting in perfect harmony with the handler provides to them both as they work seemingly effortlessly as a team can readily communicate itself to almost any spectator like an electric current. Because, of necessity, most work between dog and handler is unseen, such moments are more often something shared simply between handler and dog, or between huntsman and hounds, which in itself provides an enduring bond between them. It is understandable, however, why after many such privately shared moments an owner would wish to perpetuate the working characteristics of a dog or bitch. Even a very few such shared moments of understanding and harmony between handler and dog can be enough to form a lasting bond between them and a wish to have a lasting tie in the shape of a pup of that bloodline.

It is for this reason that many litters are bred from dogs which the show fraternity would regard as far from perfect and only the owner seems to consider desirable. It would, of course, be highly desirable if the best working characteristics could always be found in the perfect exterior. The Bernard Shaw comment once again comes to mind. While a well put together disease free animal recognisably within the breed specifications is always desirable, a good temperament, good working abilities, the desire to please and excel, to work in harmony with the handler and achieve a perfect working partnership, each playing his or her part to the full, is understandably a combination that once achieved, even if only partly, any dog owner would wish to experience again.

Sadly it is not given to many to have the opportunity, and there is usually one irreplaceable dog in every successful working dog owner's life, but by breeding with care it should be possible over several generations to get near to owning the perfect dog or bitch. This is the aim, or holy grail, to which the determined breeder aspires and if they can attain somewhere near it they will be more than satisfied. Unfortunately it is in a misdirected attempt to achieve this aim by inbreeding or by breeding from faulty stock that so much damage has been done to many breeds.

In the interests of sound breeding it is vital to stick by the rules and avoid any such mistakes as far as possible. In any event, if you do decide to breed, then good luck with your choice of dog and bitch, with your mating and the birth and rearing of your litter, and may they bring pleasure to you and their owners. Although it is only too easily forgotten, that in the end is what it should all be about.

Chapter 1 | WHAT IS INVOLVED

It is clearly undesirable to keep a working dog in a city. Yet unfortunately around all the larger cities in these islands the countryside is changing rapidly. What used to be thriving villages, filled with country people contributing to the agricultural life surrounding them, as craftsmen and skilled workers such as ditch diggers, fence layers, mechanics and part time farm workers, have changed radically as everything has been mechanised and there are few jobs available in the countryside. The village shop has had to close, often along with the village pub. The rectory has been sold to a city businessman, whose wife and daughters ride horses round the lanes. The village houses are occupied by retired couples or city workers who commute to their country home only at the weekends. The old squire has sold up to a TV celebrity or a footballer who is seldom at home.

The village is now metamorphosed into a multi-cultural enclave in the country whose inhabitants' interests are almost entirely based in the city where they work and who merely see the countryside as somewhere for them to relax by their swimming pool, while their children ride their ponies. The remaining farmers' incomes are shrinking, and they are only surviving by taking in bed-and-breakfast visitors or otherwise diversifying. Is it surprising that the country way of life is vanishing along with the skylarks and other threatened species now that all the major conurbations are surrounded by sterile enclaves of this kind? Is it surprising that genuine working dogs are becoming less common? Their way of life in many areas, like that of their owners, is under threat and slowly vanishing.

This may appear a pessimistic and iconoclastic view of life in Britain but certainly the question to ask yourself initially is whether you are really in a position to keep a bitch and breed from it. This may seem superfluous if you already have a bitch, but breeding is a serious business, not something to be entered into lightly. So, for that matter, is owning a dog or a bitch in the first place, yet many people do not seem to realise that ownership of any animal also entails responsibility for it. Owning a dog should mean that you are ready and able to provide it with a reasonable living space of its

English Springer Spaniel and her puppies (Carol Ann Johnson)

own, whether a basket in a special corner or an outside kennel. It also means that you should be prepared to train your dog up to a reasonable standard of behaviour and provide it with regular exercise preferably at least twice a day. Regular meals of more than just scraps or leftovers and a supply of water always on hand are also essential. Nor should a dog be left for long periods cooped up in a kennel or room by itself without company of any sort. Those are just some of the more obvious basics too often skimped or overlooked.

If you are proposing to breed you must realise that much more is required. You should have space enough indoors or out to allow the bitch a warm and roomy area for whelping in complete privacy. Preferably you should also have sufficient space to allow the mother and pups access to a reasonable run outside as the pups begin to develop. You, or someone delegated to by you whom you can trust entirely, are also going to need to spend a good deal of time looking after them. They cannot just be left to themselves unattended for long periods. You have acted as God and brought the puppies into the world and they are your responsibility.

Those are just the obvious preliminary requirements, but there are many more, which many people find themselves unable to fulfil. That is why each year literally thousands of unwanted dogs have to be put down by vets around the country. Many dog owners simply do not exercise their dogs regularly or supervise them properly. Such irresponsible owners allow their dogs to roam freely. In these circumstances naturally the dogs mate and have unwanted mongrel litters which mostly cannot be sold and have to be put down. That is why the vast majority of vets who have to perform this unpleasant task are in favour of spaying bitches and neutering dogs that are not specifically required for breeding.

The next question to ask yourself is why go to all the trouble of breeding? Numerous litters of almost every breed of working dog, as well as a fair selection of cross-bred animals, are advertised for sale each year so the inevitable question arises. Why bother to breed when you can simply buy a puppy from apparently guaranteed good working stock? It might even be argued that you are simply adding to an already overstocked market for no really valid reason.

Like everything else, of course, the guarantee of 'good working stock', in common with many other similar guarantees, is subject to many sub-clauses. As in any contract of sale, it is always desirable to read the small print closely, by which time you frequently find the 'cast-iron' guarantee is not worth the paper on which it is written. There are undoubtedly many good sound working puppies to be had in the open market but unless you know their background and are certain of their breeding and quality you are probably well advised to have a care. There are also a great many indifferent puppies advertised for sale as having been bred by kennels with seemingly glowing testimonials and lists of awards, which in practice are very often little better than puppy farms.

If you have the space and are sure you have the commitment it may therefore be validly argued that in breeding from your own bitch, which you know to be reasonable, while not necessarily claiming her to be excellent, you are at least working with the devil you know, rather than the devil you don't. You may also know of a likely sire that you have seen working, have liked the look of, and which you feel would mate well with your bitch. If you have personal knowledge of such a dog you may very well feel justified in considering putting the two together and breeding puppies by him from your own bitch. By even thinking on these lines you are certainly on the slippery slope and already well on the way to doing so.

You must understand, however,

1. that by preparing to breed a litter you are making a long term commitment;

2. that you are about to subject yourself and those around you to an undertaking which will almost certainly mean several months of differing degrees of stress, the results of which may be with you for years;

3. that you have to be prepared to go into the matter thoroughly and once started must be completely resolved to go through with it come what may;

4. that you must be ready to spend the considerable time and trouble that is certain to be involved;

5. that you have to be ready to do as well as you possibly can by your bitch and her litter once they are born;

6. that you must be prepared to put up with setbacks and disasters and at times utter mayhem, including the dire possibility of losing your bitch and the pups if things go really badly wrong.

If you cannot face up to any or all of these then do not breed.

Finally, purely on the economic side, it is advisable to consider the matter carefully, for breeding can be an expensive business and you may end up considerably out of pocket. You may even in the worst possible scenario lose the mother and the pups as well, ending up with not only no litter but no bitch either, as well as being very much worse off financially. Veterinary fees are often high and still have to be paid even when the worst happens. In this instance it is a case of 'if you can't take the heat then don't even go into the kitchen'.

The costs of breeding a litter are, in any event, likely to be considerable and are not always easily foreseen. For a start the stud fee itself may be large, usually at least the likely price of a pup from the expected litter. It may often be a good deal more, depending on the breeding and record of the chosen dog both in his work and as a sire. However, it may be that the owner likes the bitch's appearance, working ability and pedigree and is prepared to accept the pup of their choice from the litter in lieu of a fee. The latter is normally a safe option for the owner of the sire because if the litter is successful their dog's reputation as a sire is enhanced and if it is only mediocre they can blame the bitch. Either way they have only one pup to sell as opposed to a whole litter. Even if it does not turn out as well as might have been hoped they can probably afford the time to keep it and sell it as a trained, or partly trained, dog at a very much enhanced price.

Where the stud fee is waived in favour of a pup from the litter true accounting should debit the cost of that pup against the cost of the litter. Even if all goes well, however, the vet's fees are still likely to be considerable, at least the cost of another pup or even several more, depending on whether there are any problems with the pregnancy. If the breed is one where testing for hip dysplasia and eyesight problems is necessary this in itself is an expensive business necessarily adding to the costs involved. Complications in the pregnancy, emergency call outs, costs of a Caesarean, possibly resulting in the loss of some or all of the litter or even the bitch herself, the costs of injections, micro-chipping, or tattooing, along with the KC registration fees for the pups, all quickly mount up alarmingly and will all have to be deducted from the price finally obtained for those pups sold.

It is thus very easy to see that if the litter is only a small one of two or three pups, instead of making anything by breeding from the bitch there may be a considerable financial loss involved. This does not include the necessary costs of extra feeding and the time and care spent on looking after the bitch and pups. Lastly, although after the litter has arrived the time for this should already be long past, there are the costs of advertising the pups and other expenses such as telephone calls connected with their sales which can all mount up alarmingly before the pups are sold and finally depart.

All in all any prospective breeder should consider the profit and debit side and ask themselves whether it is really worth the hassle and expense which will almost certainly be involved. After anything like an accurate summary of the true costs involved, always including the time and labour of the breeder, the honest answer must usually be that it is not even worth considering financially. This, however, will not stop those who are hell bent on breeding from their bitch. As far as novice breeders go the only reasonable comment is that there is one born every minute. Yet it should also be admitted that the satisfaction of seeing a pup you have bred from your own bitch performing well in the field is considerable and many would regard it as worth all the time, trouble and expense involved.

Greyhound puppies and bitch (Carol Ann Johnson)

If you are prepared to go into the matter wholeheartedly and regardless of anything else spend the necessary time and effort to do your best for your bitch, prior to and through the whole breeding process, as well as look after the puppies and their welfare – if you are prepared to spare the time, the considerable trouble and the heartbreak almost certainly involved, in return for the hope of possibly having the satisfaction of seeing a pup, or pups, of your own breeding working as well, if not better, than their dam – then go ahead and breed, but make sure you go into it thoroughly and know what you are doing and what to expect.

Those foolish enough to decide to breed simply because their bitch is in season and their neighbours have a nice looking dog of the same variety are simply asking for trouble and will probably end up considerably out of pocket, but, even if sadder, at least no doubt a little the wiser. Only those who happen to own a dog or a bitch and who decide to buy a pup of the opposite sex then find themselves breeding, either intentionally, or willy-nilly, may be regarded as more misguided, but even if the lesson is learned the hard way, at least they too should have been taught the basic facts of life.

If you are thinking seriously of breeding from your bitch then, although it is often overlooked, the sensible thing to do is to first find out whether she is fit to breed. A thorough veterinary examination to check out her breeding potential should be the basic first step of anyone thinking of possibly putting their bitch in pup. A thorough check on heart, lungs, and general health should be covered. In addition, any necessary tests for hereditary weaknesses such as hip dysplasia, cataracts, incipient blindness and inturning eyelids should also be covered if this has not already been done. If you are to be strict about such matters the cost of this should also be first entry on the debit side against the cost of the prospective litter. Only when your bitch has been thoroughly examined and passed as fit to have a litter should you start considering the next stage. It is surprising, however, how many people completely overlook this really vitally important first step.

Having hopefully got the all-clear from the vet regarding the health of the bitch as a prospective mother the next step may not cost you anything but is likely to be a great deal more difficult because before breeding from her it is necessary to make an honest assessment of her as a working dog. However hard you may find it to do so – and most owners find it extremely difficult – it is essential be honest with yourself and look seriously for her weak points, as well as any hereditary defects which make it less desirable to breed from her such as bad ratings for hip dysplasia or cataracts. Is her temperament, biddability and willingness to please all you would wish for? Is her conformation good all round or has she some aspects which could be improved? Is her working ability first rate, or, for instance, are her nose and mouth not as good as you might wish? Having decided on her weaknesses by all means balance them with her strong points, but try not to delude yourself, as is so easily done. Then start looking for a dog which is strong on her weak points and which hopefully will, for instance, add bone, stamina, drive, nose, temperament or other qualities which you are prepared to acknowledge could improve the all round abilities you are looking for in your bitch's progeny.

However hard it may be, the more honest you are about your bitch's weaknesses the better the progeny are likely to be if the chosen sire is strong in those respects. This same balanced judgement should, of course, as far as possible be applied to the prospective sire, but it is not always easy to make such assessments fully unless you have the opportunity to watch him working over quite a lengthy period. Such assessments often have to be made over a short period and largely on the past records of the dog's success at work and as a sire. These records are, unfortunately, almost inevitably only available on paper and the true facts may be somewhat different. A field trial may be won, for instance, because that particular day went well and the opposition was poor, not because the dog was outstanding. Progeny may have done well because the bitch was outstanding rather than the sire. If, however, you have the chance to view past litters he has sired and assess the general standard of the pups in two or three different litters that could be a more telling factor in your choice of the prospective sire.

Snap judgements may sometimes have to be made, but it is never advisable just to choose any dog simply because it happens to be readily available. That is a mistake which is easily made, but it is also one that is often regretted after the event. The sire, it is worth repeating, should be chosen as far as possible to be complementary in every way to the bitch so that the progeny may hopefully be better in most respects. This is of course somewhat obviously the counsel of perfection. Furthermore it is not always guaranteed to be successful. That is one of the pitfalls of breeding. What are apparently the best matching sire and dam on paper or to the eye of the prospective breeder may not always produce the best progeny. There is always an element of luck involved which may be good or bad.

It is worth always bearing in mind that what may be termed the 'Bernard Shaw and the actress syndrome' may to some extent come into operation when the opposite was intended. Long forgotten ancestors in the background of the dog or bitch may have had legs like Bernard Shaw and brains like the actress, genes which have unexpectedly recurred. It is therefore always desirable to know your antecedents as far back as possible when breeding. Close inbreeding is something to be avoided in general but breeding from sound bloodlines and trying for compatability in both sire and dam's pedigrees is always desirable.

A close look at sire and dam, and preferably their sires and dams if possible, should give anyone with a good eye some concept of how the progeny might turn out. The appearance of similar apparently good bloodlines in both sire and dam's backgrounds should indicate that you are following a worthwhile trail already blazed by others, but is desirable to learn as much as you can about them. Some apparently outstanding records are not necessarily as good as they appear on paper. Both obituaries and pedigrees can be extremely misleading. It is always worthwhile, however, to strive for what appears to be improvement regardless of possible pitfalls and even if perfection is still some way away.

Finding a really suitable sire is, however, only the first stage in a lengthy process. It is necessary to know that he will be available when your bitch is coming into season. Knowing any more than the likely month or quarter when this is due is about the best that can usually be done in advance. Then, when the bitch does come into season, it is necessary to watch her very carefully and choose the right moment to introduce her to the sire. The problems of breeding are legion and this initial problem can be extremely frustrating. Nature can never be tied down to exact deadlines or be relied on to follow what are considered suitable timings.

Whether the dog is taken to the bitch or the bitch to the dog is a matter for you and the sire's owner to decide. If you are proposing to take the bitch to a professional kennel owner or established breeder they will almost certainly wish to know details of the bitch, her pedigree and her working potential and something about you yourself, your experience of the breed and working the dogs, and how well you are likely to cope with the litter.

If you are a novice breeder and are sensible enough to admit it and put yourself in their hands to some extent and ask their advice they will almost certainly be very helpful, as it is in their own interests that the litter, if they approve of your bitch, should reflect well on their dog as sire. They will probably prefer to have the bitch to stay in their kennels because this more or less ensures that she will be covered, i.e. mated, at the right times. It may be, however, that they will prefer to bring their dog to your bitch, if only to examine your kennelling arrangements initially and possibly suggest bringing the bitch back to them for a second mating or vice versa.

If, however, the owner of the dog is not a professional kennel owner but an amateur inexperienced in the mechanics of mating and this is the first occasion for you and the bitch as well, then it is highly desirable for both of you to find someone with experience to assist the pair of you because it is not a process that is necessarily either easy or quick. Covering a bitch is not something that should be taken lightly at any stage and it can be difficult to ensure that the timing is right for two consecutive matings with the gap of a day between them which is normally considered desirable.

If the timing is wrong the intended mating may easily be a complete failure, with even an experienced sire unable to cover the bitch. If the season is over there is no way that a mating can be successful. On the other hand it may be that only one mating can be accomplished successfully and the second cannot be consummated, with the consequent possibility of a less successful litter. The importance of getting the timing absolutely correct makes clear the advantage of the bitch and the dog being together in the same kennels during the critical mating period.

Assuming, however, that all has gone well at this stage and the mating has gone according to plan and been a complete success, this is merely

Two Flatcoated Retriever puppies enjoying a game (Carol Ann Johnson)

the start of a lengthy process going on for anything from six months to a lifetime. It all depends on whether this first experience is enough to convince the breeder that this is a one-off event or something to be repeated. The likelihood is that it will be one or the other as breeding is something which some people find traumatic, even revolting, at almost every stage while others find it immensely satisfying. This total divide between novice breeders is quite common from the planning stage right through to the arrival of the litter, and even seeing them off to their new homes; a moment that cannot come too soon for most first-time breeders.

Either way, successful or only partially successful, the mating is just the start of a lengthy procedure involving much necessary expense and upheaval. It is important, for instance, as mentioned earlier, to have a suitable kennel space for the prospective mother and her puppies when they are born. A whelping bed, or box of suitable proportions, big enough to allow the bitch to lie freely at full length for delivering the pups, in a secluded area, is desirable. This need not take up a large amount of space, however, and almost anywhere, within reason, can be adapted for the purpose.

Later, however, a run will be required for the bitch and puppies once the puppies have been successfully delivered and reared to this stage. These should all have been prepared and made ready well in advance of the arrival of the litter. Forward planning is essential at each stage of the proceedings and it is essential to know what will be required well in advance. If this is equipment that has to be acquired or made, even though it need not be costly, it is yet another expense that should be set against the price of the pups.

The bitch should naturally enough be watched and worked with care during her pregnancy. Because she is feeding the puppies it is desirable to feed and exercise her with due care, like any pregnant mother. It is unnecessary to pamper her unduly, but after the first few weeks any excessive work or unduly strenuous exercise is undesirable, although within reason she may be exercised and worked normally. While seeing she is well fed it is also desirable to make sure that she does not get too fat. In most cases all should go perfectly smoothly, but an eye should naturally be kept on her general health for signs such as a staring coat, unusually dark or loose faeces, and anything untoward, especially any sign of bleeding or discharge.

If you do have any worries about the bitch it is probably desirable to take her to the vet for a check. There is no harm in having a professional opinion on how the pregnancy is going – in fact it is sensible to do so. For the novice breeder the more assurances available that everything is progressing naturally, the better. It is better to know in advance that all is well rather than find out the hard way that something is seriously wrong or that obvious precautions or preparations have been forgotten or ignored.

It may also be desired to have a scan arranged to know for certain whether the mating has been a success and the bitch is actually in pup. Anyway, if at no other time, the vet's services will be required once the pups are born to remove the dew claws as well as possibly to dock the tails and give them a reassuring check over. It will be necessary also before they depart to their new owners to register them with the Kennel Club and they will require their preliminary injections. It may also be desired to insert microchips or tattoo them for identification, all of which is of course adding to the expense.

There is absolutely no way that several visits to the vet can be avoided, even if it may not be necessary to call him or her out on more than a limited number of occasions, and these necessary charges are yet further items to be added to the mounting costs of the pups. Breeding is necessarily an expensive business and not all litters, by any means, are sold at a price which begins to compensate for the time, effort and overall outlay involved. Indeed, if the pups are not sold before they are weaned the breeder may easily find the expenditure far outweighing any possible returns.

When the breeder is left with two or three hungry growing pups unsold he or she will find the cost of keeping them spiralling by the week, and may well end up in desperation trying to give them away and finding that even this is difficult. This, it might be added, is no exaggeration and by no means an unusual state of affairs where there has been a sudden rush of puppies advertised on the market at the same time. After an experience such as that the novice breeder is unlikely to wish to repeat the performance, but such breeders have only themselves to blame.

All the preparations for breeding pups already mentioned, including finding suitable good homes for them, should ideally be made before the mating has even taken place. It is certainly arguable that being assured of good homes in advance for any puppies that may be forthcoming from a mating should be one of the primary aims of any breeder. Indeed it might even be argued that the mating is one of the last stages in the process of breeding pups, even if it is admittedly an essential part of it.

It is highly desirable that anyone preparing to breed knows in advance what to expect and what pitfalls may lie in the way and how best to avoid them. That is the object of this book and if it does help in this way to any extent then it has been worthwhile. Certainly novice breeders should find that they have saved the price of the book several times over by the time they have bred and sold their pups, simply by avoiding some of the common oversights which are very easily overlooked or forgotten by the breeder who is simply prepared to leave it all to Mother Nature and trust to luck. Breeding is a serious business and there is no place for the innocent amateur who is not prepared to take it seriously. He or she deserves all the problems they will undoubtedly encounter.

Of course even where all has gone well and sire and dam seem to have been perfectly matched the breeder cannot be sure that the litter has been successful in the early days after they have been satisfactorily delivered. It takes time for the pups to mature and show their full potential. There are, however, immediate signs by which some measure of how successful the breeding has been may be measured. For example, the more even the litter the more generally successful it is likely to have been.

A litter with widely differing sizes or with any malformed pups may provide one or two good dogs or bitches, but an even litter with a selection of good types true to the breed or to the dam or sire is much preferable. It is more obvious proof of a well matched and successful mating, quite apart, of course, from being much more saleable. If there were three couplings when mating, however, there may well be some pups obviously smaller than the others in a large litter, because they may be four days younger and this should be taken into account.

Size at birth, however, usually provides as good a guide as any to the success of the mating. Indeed to the experienced eye the pups at birth can provide a very good idea of how the mating has resulted. As the pups grow older, if they are not fed separately or watched and weighed carefully, greedy feeders and more dominant dogs or bitches can readily grow ahead of their siblings. Thus at six to eight weeks the pups in a litter may sometimes begin to seem very different in size whereas at birth they were a very even selection. The longer they remain even, however, the better the mating and their care has probably been.

The first breeding over, successfully or not, the novice breeders may, of course, decide that it is not an experience they ever wish to repeat. Hopefully, however, they will have been successful and decided that in due course they wish to repeat the process. If they can steadily produce better progeny of their own breeding over the years that is something well worth aiming at and, if they are successful in even a minor way, something to be proud of indeed. If they are only keeping their own bloodline going successfully and are seeing the same characteristics appearing in successive generations over the years this is something which in itself can give enormous satisfaction. Short of cloning your favourite dog or bitch it is the next best thing, and possibly even more satisfying. A pup which is undoubtedly better than its dam and/or sire should be the aim of the breeder, rather than simply another just the same. It is, however, not something easily achieved.

To see a puppy showing all the characteristics you recall her dam showing, and even going on to outdo her on occasions can be very pleasing indeed. To see a youngster performing well and eclipsing her dam or granddams is also extremely gratifying. The same is, of course, true of a male pup compared with his sire or grandsires. Even to see them simply showing the same quirks of character is pleasing to watch. Really excellent work in the field seen only by the breeders themselves, with a satisfying sense of inner warmth, are amongst the hidden rewards of breeding successfully over the years. Although they may stand as a tangible measure of the breeder's success, the outright rewards, the field trial successes or excellent work in the field observed by others and duly applauded are often really less important than those treasured private memories.

Having once bred successfully, of course, the temptation is to repeat the process. Just bear in mind that next time everything may not go according to plan or as smoothly as on the previous occasion. Inevitably there will be setbacks and unforeseen problems, often when least expected. If, however, you are prepared to take the time and trouble involved over the years then you deserve a measure of success and will probably achieve it at least to some degree. It is, however, a long-term business that is measured in decades rather than years and it demands a long term view. Breeding dogs, like breeding any livestock, requires determination, a good eye for an animal, a good nerve and above all perseverance. Whether you choose to do it professionally or as an amateur, just remember that luck plays a large part in every successful mating, but that with care and advance planning a good deal of the uncertainty involved can be avoided and the odds can be considerably stacked in your favour.

Chapter 2 | THE INITIAL STAGES

Bitches tend to come into season at about six monthly intervals, but this is by no means a hard and fast rule. The first season may be at six or even nine months and may be hardly noticeable. It is usually, however, unmistakable. In the classic case the vulva will gradually begin to swell noticeably and the bitch will probably soon be licking it frequently. Thereafter the bitch may start to show signs of colour, i.e dark red blood, and leave large or small patches behind her despite fairly steady licking. The process may go on for two or three days, a week, or even longer in some cases.

The bitch should come into season, or begin the cycle of oestrus, at between six and twelve months old, thereafter continuing at six to eight month intervals. After around ten days of the oestrus she should begin ovulating, i.e. producing eggs in the ovaries, and stop showing colour, and she will become receptive to the dog. The period between the seasons, known as the anoestrus period, is usually fairly constant once started but varies between bitches considerably The period after the eggs have been fertilised in the uterus is known as the metoestrus period, and within approximately sixty-three days the pups should arrive.

In a few bitches the season may be so short and brief that it may even be missed altogether unless the owner is watching out for it closely. There are, of course, numerous medical conditions which may cause irregular seasons such as cystic ovaries and similar problems with the reproductive organs. If this is considered a possibility then a visit to the vet is indicated if only for peace of mind and to prove all is well. Normally the blood will flow richly and red to start with, turning slowly to a paler colour before it finally stops after nine or ten days.

If the first season is plain to see then the second is likely to follow in a six-monthly cycle and so on, but here again there are frequently tiresome variations with individual bitches. Sometimes a bitch which has seemed quite regular may suddenly change completely. There are other bitches that are simply irregular, or even seem to miss a part of the cycle completely.

Teaser at work: Border terrier showing bitch in season and ready to mate. Her tail is curling and she is standing firmly as he licks her vulva

Some bitches, on the other hand, seem to remain in season for several weeks while others have hardly started before it is apparently all over. Especially in some younger bitches it can be very tiresomely erratic.

The average bitch, however, should be fairly regular and should show colour effectively for eleven days. That, or something close to it, should be the normal pattern, but as always in anything to do with dogs, especially female dogs, there are frequent inexplicable exceptions to the expected routine. In any event, if you wish to breed from your bitch it is always advisable to watch her carefully over the periods when she might normally be expected to come into season so that you can establish a pattern early on and know when to start looking for tell-tale signs. Unfortunately the average novice breeder is usually rather inept at observing the cycle accurately, failing to spot when it really first showed signs of starting. This is easily enough done, but it can lead to highly inaccurate forecasts of when she is ready to mate with a prospective sire.

If, of course, you have a dog as well as your bitch, or are in regular contact with a dog, their behaviour should very quickly inform you when the bitch is coming into season and when she is ready to mate. The difficulty then may be keeping them separate to avoid breeding, unless the dog is neutered. Even then it is probably kinder to them both to keep them separate as the dog will probably be constantly pursuing the bitch and attempting to couple with her. Then, unfortunately, if they are kept apart, he will probably be very vocal in his misery. It is almost inevitably a difficult period for all concerned.

If the bitch is apparently slow in coming into season, or the seasons are particularly difficult to detect, then keeping her in company with a dog is usually sufficient to bring on a full season, but it is of course desirable to make sure that in such circumstances a mating does not occur accidentally. While letting Nature encourage the bitch to ovulate fully it is not necessarily desirable to complete the process. Keeping unneutered dogs together with entire bitches can be a tricky business at such times unless they can be conveniently kennelled separately.

Many owners who do not intend to breed favour spaying a bitch at an early age to prevent the inevitable mess around the house and avoid the unwanted attentions of male dogs. It is certainly true that if you have a dog, or worse still dogs, as well as a bitch and wish to keep them together you are inevitably going to have problems. The regular trauma every six months or so when the bitch comes into season means that she has then to be kept separate at all times. The dog, or dogs, inevitably howl their frustration throughout the two or three weeks (or more) involved and may well fight even if normally the best of friends.

If any misalliance should occur and a dog and bitch accidentally mate it is important if they have reached the stage of becoming locked together that no attempt is made to separate them as this may lead to serious injury. It is necessary to wait until they separate naturally, when there are several possible solutions. If it is not desired to breed from her the bitch can be spayed, which solves the problem, if rather drastically and permanently. She can alternatively be given an immediate dose of oestrogen, which, although it may be effective in neutralising the mating, is undesirable as it is not likely to be good for her long term health and may make breeding at a later date more difficult. It is probably wisest to wait and see whether the coupling has been successful and, if it has resulted in pregnancy, then a better solution for the bitch is to abort her medically, which is likely to be effective and less drastic.

All this is probably enough to persuade many owners of the advantages of spaying or neutering, but either, if done at all, should be done early and

Greyhound bitch showing every sign of being ready to mate (Jackie Drakeford)

there is no reversing the decision once the operation has been performed. As a breeder I am against spaying or neutering simply for the owner's convenience. In any instance, however, where dogs and bitches are being kept together and individual kennelling is not available, preferably some distance apart at that, it has to be admitted that it is probably the sensible solution. While professional kennels are equipped to cope with this situation many amateur breeders without unlimited room for their dogs probably find it difficult.

It really is only sensible to keep dogs of the opposite sex if you have suitable kennelling arrangements and are able to ensure that they can be kept separate when required. Otherwise there is always the danger of a misalliance and an unwanted litter, possibly of crossbred puppies. However close an eye may be kept on a bitch when she is running freely in the company of a dog or dogs, it is always possible that somehow they have managed to breed, even though you were unaware that she was coming into season. Alternatively some dogs can be escape artists and capable of outdoing Houdini when it comes to breaking out of or into apparently secure kennels, or seizing on any momentary lapse of concentration on the part of their owner. It is amazing how easy it is to breed unintentionally when you have dogs of the opposite sex, especially when you consider how difficult it can be at times when you actually intend it to happen.

There are naturally some dog owners who simply do not have room available for separate kennelling. For them, spaying the bitch or neutering the dog may be the only solution. Even owners who have plenty of room may feel that neutering a single dog when there are several bitches may solve the problem of keeping them all together in the house. It is easier then to feed and exercise them all together and avoid tiresome segregation when a bitch comes into season.

Of course there are also those idle owners who neuter or spay their only dog or bitch simply for their own convenience as a matter of course. They are usually the same owners who cease to exercise those same dogs or bitches as much, if at all, when the shooting season is over and spend their time instead playing occasional rounds of golf or indulging in rather more sedentary pursuits. Their animals are usually overweight and stolid looking beasts anchored during each shoot to their owners and only allowed to retrieve the occasional dead bird. As they are probably overfed and under-exercised, such beasts are, like their owners, more likely to have heart attacks than puppies, and it is probably best that they are not considered as prospective dams or sires. Dog owners of this kind are only excelled by those who regularly have their animals put down when they go on holiday and then buy a replacement on their return,. Every vet will know dog owners such as these.

Assuming that all is well with your bitch, however, and that you wish to breed, it should be a reasonably straightforward process. If she is coming into season normally and regularly there should be little or no problem in estimating an approximate date when you may wish to mate her with the dog of your choice. Given complete freedom of choice in the matter it is probably easier and preferable to choose a mating at a date which ensures that the pups are born in late spring or early summer. In this case they can be reasonably sure to enjoy good warm weather outdoors during their formative months rather than being confined indoors during wet or cold wintry weather. Of course outside factors are always involved which may make such a mating impossible or, in the breeder's view, undesirable.

There are some compelling reasons why a litter born early in the year may be considered more desirable than one born late in the year. For instance, the Kennel Club in assessing ages starts from January 1 each year so that a pup born in December may therefore be expected to compete against a pup born eleven months earlier, and hence is clearly at a disadvantage. Thus a keen competitor in field trials, shows or other events might well consider that a pup born early in the year is worth more than a pup born late in the year, although this advantage may only persist over the early years of the animal's life. Viewed dispassionately, however, a pup born in February and reared outside in a warm March and April would undoubtedly do as well, if not better than a pup born in October and reared in a cold and gloomy November and December. In general the spring is probably preferable to the autumn or winter months for rearing pups. It is, unfortunately, not always easy to pick and choose when the pups should arrive because breeding frequently depends entirely on the vagaries of the bitch coming into season at whatever time suits her.

Of course some smaller breeds, such as working terriers, may only have two to four pups in a litter and can be readily managed mostly indoors. A larger breed such as a Labrador, on the other hand, with a litter of eight or ten will require much more room. They will preferably need a good-sized outdoor run as they are approaching being weaned, whereas the smaller litter may be perfectly all right mainly indoors and with access to a small run outside.

Then again there is often a considerable variation in weather patterns between the north and the south of the UK. Thus a breeder in the south may expect a mild and reasonably warm winter, as opposed to someone in the north where it may be persistently freezing cold and wet. In the main, though, whether the litter is large or small, in the north or in the south, the principle that the spring or summer months are generally better for rearing young puppies cannot really be gainsaid.

It also has to be taken into account that different breeds develop at different rates, and while some may be near full grown and ready to breed by eighteen months old, other breeds are barely fully grown at two or sometimes even three years of age. Taking around eighteen months to two years as a reasonable age at which to have the first litter, however, the pattern of the bitch's seasons should by this time have been established. If the bitch has been short and irregular, having her first seasons at six months and a year, it is probably advisable to introduce her to a dog as the time for the eighteen month season approaches to try to ensure a fuller and more natural reaction when it is desired to breed,

The novice breeder should also avoid the mistake of leaving it all too late. It is probably preferable to breed from the bitch at two or three years old rather than leave it to three or four. If for some reason the mating is not successful, which may happen through no fault of the bitch, she will then be six months older when the next mating can take place. If this mating again fails for some reason, or alternatively produces a very successful litter so that a year or so later you wish to breed from her again, by then her age may be against it.

Breeding from a bitch of eight years old, even if she has not been worked hard, is something probably better avoided, although some bitches are fit enough for it and have had litters at this age or even later. It is, however, certainly better not to breed for the first time when anywhere near approaching this age. The Kennel Club may refuse to register the progeny of a bitch mated at eight or over.

The question of age is not the only matter affecting mating, of course, and although important is by no means all important. Hereditary defects such as hip dysplasia and eye problems that may cause blindness, such as PRA (Progressive Retinal Atrophy), which are unfortunately endemic in some breeds, may be so bad in a particular dog or bitch that the breed societies may advise against breeding from them. Unfortunately, of course, they cannot prevent people from breeding and selling their pups if they are not registered with the Kennel Club or are not members of the breed society. The result is that such hereditary defects sometimes continue to spread despite the best efforts of registered breeders and the Kennel Club.

The question of temperament is to my mind equally, if not even more important than hereditary defects. Unless the bitch has a reasonably calm temperament it is probably undesirable to consider breeding from her in the first place. To breed from a bitch in the hope that having pups will calm her down is almost certainly a recipe for disaster. A highly strung bitch may be considered as undesirable to breed from, if not more so, than a bitch with an obvious deformity such as very bad hip dysplasia, a very undershot or overshot jaw, or other abnormalities. Apart from anything else the mating itself could well be fraught with trouble. 'Hysteria' was for a brief post-war period not uncommon amongst some highly inbred dogs amounting in some cases to near insanity. In a very few, mostly non-working, breeds it could easily have become a considerable problem but has now been virtually eradicated. It is certainly something to be avoided at all costs.

Temperament is undoubtedly of primary concern in a working dog, but it covers a very broad spectrum and is also somewhat difficult to define. Dogs are often said to have a calm or a highly strung temperament but there is really much more to it than that in a good working dog. A perfect working temperament implies a dog with drive, knowledge of its job and a natural inborn understanding of what is required, as well as a willingness to please, calmness under stress, boldness when required, and an intuitive partnership with its handler so that the two work as a team. Clearly such perfection is rare but a dog with a good working temperament which responds well to its handler and understands readily what is expected of it when working is well on the way to achieving it.

Such natural biddability and willingness to please should certainly be regarded as a huge plus factor. It is undoubtedly one of the foremost qualities to look for in any working dog or bitch. Any regularly worked dog which has daily experience in the field and learns to work happily in conjunction with its handler will in the course of its lifetime almost certainly develop much of the temperament required, even if it is not necessarily perfect. Temperament, as thus defined in a working dog is something that undoubtedly improves with experience.

A dog which never works as it is intended to do inevitably loses much as a result. Such dogs are often said to be highly strung or to have a nervous temperament. Their chief problem is usually that they are being kept in a town or city, possibly in a flat where they are left for long periods at a time without access to the outside world. They do not have any real outlets for their natural working skills and they naturally become nervous, highly strung and temperamental. The gap between them and working dogs of the same breed which have daily experience of all the sorts of tasks required of them as a matter of course is quite understandably immense. Their temperaments are bound to be different. The one has a regular outlet for its instincts and the other is permanently stifled and constrained.

In the same way it can also be said that the gap between the temperaments of owners may also be immense. Different owners may have widely disparate views on almost everything from politics to religion, as well as having totally different backgrounds and ambitions, quite apart from living in completely different environments and having completely different lifestyles. Their views on life and how to live it may be as different as their own temperaments and those of their dogs. The environment to a large extent moulds the owner and the dog.

Working each day in a city office and returning each evening to the confines of a flat is sadly almost totally incompatible with owning a working dog. However much their owners may try to exercise them, this fact is generally reflected in any such unfortunate dog's behaviour. Some city-dwelling dog owners, particularly those who have weekend country retreats, like to claim that they have the best of both worlds, but whether their dogs would agree with them is another matter.

On such occasions I am somehow reminded of a self-styled gundog trainer I met many years ago. He was a rough and ready type of a kind probably common enough in the nineteenth century, with rough and ready dogs which he dealt with accordingly. Perhaps fortunately he was not the sort of individual often encountered even then, but he was not without a sense of humour of a naturally somewhat sardonic kind. When I first met him he explained to me that he had recently been looking for a guard dog for his kennels, because he lived some distance from them, in itself a rather strange admission, as was his tale of how he acquired and 'trained' his guard dog.

'A lad came up to me and said "I hear you're looking for a sharp dog for your kennels. Well, I've got one. He's too sharp for me and you can have him for nowt."

'So I looks at the dog and he were nobbut shaggy awld mongrel and I claps him all over and he seems alright, so I says, "Thanks very much" and after I've done dogs I chains him up in doorway and leaves him for night. In morning when I comes down to kennels he's standing in doorway and when I bends down to clap him he nearly takes arm off. So I says. "You needs more than clapping, you do." So I picks up a stob which I see lying handy and clouts him with it behind lughole. I looks down to see he's still breathing like and goes on in and does dogs. When I gets back he's standing up shaking his head, groggy like. And after that I don't have no more trouble with 'im.'

The gap between such an old guard gundog trainer's methods, completely outdated even half a century ago, and today's dog handlers is, of course, immense. There is, however, very little doubt that there is now also quite a considerable gap between many owners of working dogs in the country and most city dwelling dog owners. The different circumstances in which their dog are kept usually make this almost inevitable. It is difficult, if not impossible, to exercise a dog effectively in the diminishing green spaces available in most cities. Long periods spent in the confines of a town house or flat, as well as exercise in the fumes of the city streets, do not help the unfortunate dog either.

Lest it be thought that I am attacking city or town dwelling dog owners as such, let it be clear that I am not. I have a considerable admiration for anyone who has the dedication and determination to keep a dog well exercised and fit in a busy town or city, even if I cannot feel it is ultimately in the dog's best interests. I certainly do not think they should breed dogs in such circumstances, but I am impressed by anyone who can consistently clean up after their dogs have defecated, and comply with all the other by-laws inflicted on dog owners by town councils.

It was partly on this score that I had a considerable falling out with some close relations when they were living in a city flat and we had no-one available to look after our dogs. They were incensed because we refused to stay with them, but our dogs, like some others unused to towns and used to a grass run, have an aversion to urinating or defecating on concrete. As I explained, I also had an aversion, which in my case was to walking down the street to the gardens shared by the flat owners last thing at night and again in the early morning, come rain or shine, so that the dogs could relieve themselves on grass. We still agree to differ on the subject.

Unfortunately, like the gap between town and country dogs, the gap between the show dog and the working dog in most breeds is also large and growing larger every year. The breed standards for the show dog have diverged in many cases from the real working dog to a very significant degree. The poodle, which can be a very good working gundog and originated from the water dog used by Portuguese fishermen to retrieve their nets, is a commonly used example. Miniature poodles with fancy cuts and bows in their forelocks are a far cry from a standard poodle working in the field, which can be a very good gundog. This divergence between show dogs and working dogs in most working breeds is now immense. It is unfortunate, but is just one of those inevitable results of modern life as specialisation creeps insidiously into every aspect of living and as there is an ever increasing divergence between life in the cities and life in the country.

There is still in some working breeds a tenuous connection between show and working dogs. Unfortunately it is becoming steadily ever more clearly divided. There are even further divisions developing between working dogs which continue working in the way they were intended, e.g. sheepdogs that work sheep and/or cattle and those which are used solely as trial dogs and seldom if ever for working sheep or cattle, or gundogs which are only entered in working tests or in field trials and, like purely show specimens, are seldom, if ever, taken out shooting. Yet others may be used only in competitions involving balls or obstacle courses which in themselves have become specialised competitive sports.

The difference can usually be seen clearly enough. The working dog tends to look the part, perhaps slightly less well groomed but business-like and ready for work whatever it may be. The gundog eager for the working day but keeping a close eye on its handler is possibly not a perfect specimen by show standards but alert and ready for all that. The sheepdog with a keen eye on the hill and waiting for the signal to go is very different from the well turned out show specimen but is fit and can cover the hill all day. The terrier ready for the moment when it can get its jaws on a rat would probably bite anyone other than its handler. There is a clear distinction between these dogs and those of the same breeds that have no working background, and it is unlikely that any of them could win in the show ring, or in specialised competitions, although no doubt their owners do not regret the fact. They simply belong in different worlds.

The clear differences between working dogs within a single breed may thus be substantial, not to mention those which are simply kept as pets and never shown, worked or trialled. This division of working dogs into different categories within the same breed is something which any serious breeder must regret, but it has to be taken into account as, regrettably, in some breeds it has resulted in genuine working stock being very hard to find in the same way that rare breeds of cattle, pigs or poultry are sadly often kept by just a very few enthusiasts. It all makes the choice of a working sire for the person wishing to breed from a working bitch that much more difficult.

When one speaks of temperament in a working dog it is therefore important first to define the type of working dog. Is it one bred for the field, or the show ring, or as a pet, or for some other specialised activity? The dog that genuinely works in the field is a different animal from one that has been bred over generations to become the acme of perfection in the show ring or even in some working tests. Retrieving balls in competitions, while requiring a high degree of training, is after all not the ultimate aim of a collie or a retriever, and life in the confines of a town or city is not the ideal life for a working dog. Nor for that matter is training as a guide dog, a drug detector, or a guard dog, though each may be a useful, indeed invaluable, function. To learn to pose perfectly in the show ring and behave impeccably in those often testing circumstances requires very different training and temperament from those of a dog working in the field.

Over the generations, inevitably, the one form of specialised training tends to cancel out, or at the very least dull, many of the attributes required in the other. In the end one would expect the instincts to atrophy completely, but surprisingly they frequently seem merely to remain dormant. It is amazing how often, given the opportunity of working as they should do, dogs which have never previously had the chance to develop their true potential will adapt surprisingly quickly. Like battery hens that have been released from captivity they may require a considerable period of readjustment, but eventually they may regain many of their natural instincts. Unfortunately, as the years pass so the divide between working types and others tends to become greater and more difficult to overcome.

It is the temperament of the dog which is not worked as it should be which tends to suffer, especially when hip dysplasia, cataracts and other problems are present. The breeds become split between working dogs, show dogs and others to a degree where their original purpose is almost forgotten. Some of these animals become almost caricatures of the genuine working types, and far removed from what they were originally intended to be. This is what might be described as multi-purpose-ism in dogs. It should never be forgotten that we are an island race with only a steadily decreasing countryside available to a very rapidly increasing population. Dogs, like people, need sufficient space in which to work and play without being overcrowded. Working dogs also need various different types of ground as part of their working environment in order to fulfil their true potential.

Apart from space and different working environments the working dog in the field really requires what amounts to an extra sensory ability working in total harmony with its handler while using its own innate instincts to bridge the gap between the handler, itself and the animals with which they are interacting. It is almost impossible to achieve this sort of ideal combination satisfactorily with other types of work, especially in such an artificial environment as the show ring or when living in a city environment, and the gap is widening continually. Having bred dogs mainly for working and my own satisfaction, but also some who have been Champions in field trials and the show ring, and having exported successful breeding stock to Europe, the USA (Dunpender Eros, whom I bred and trained, was the All American Field Champion), South Africa and the Antipodes, (where I sent out the foundation stock of what has become one of the most popular working gundog breeds today in both Australia and New Zealand) I feel this is a matter for considerable regret, but it is also an undoubted fact of life.

The result, unfortunately, is also often reflected directly in the temperament as well as the appearance of the dogs concerned, and the working temperament and the show temperament are inevitably diverging, along with appearance, to the extent that it is recognised tacitly or overtly in many working breeds today. In some breeds, indeed, they are unwillingly accepted as distinct and separate species. This is to my mind an unfortunate and undesirable aspect of the modern trend for specialisation in almost everything but it is, however, undoubtedly a point that any would-be breeder has to take into account. Temperament as well as appearance in a working dog may be seen as a very wide-ranging matter and must be considered from widely varied aspects and angles.

The innate working instincts of any dog are, however, closer to the surface than many people may imagine. My mother-in-law had a sister who kept Pekingese. The granddam had been a show champion, albeit in the days when specialisation had not reached quite the heights it has today. The owner had bred a litter and kept two bitch pups, neither of which quite emulated their mother's show ring exploits. Each of these bitches had in turn had a litter and she had kept two pups from each. Then, somewhat late in life, she acquired a husband with a very sporting bent. He had been an MFH in his heyday but he was also a fine shot and he soon had his wife and the Pekingese completely under his control.

The entire bitch pack of seven, led by the granddam, would go out regularly with their owner's husband and his gun, starting the day impeccably brushed and groomed. Working in gorse and boggy reedy ground they would hunt out all the game to be found and enthusiastically flush it from cover. Though not great retrievers, when the game, either fur or feather, was shot, the bitches would then find it, tending to seize a leg or a wing and drag it in a rather protracted retrieve rather than pick it cleanly, but in view of their size and physiognomy this was hardly surprising. On their return from the hunt, filthy, muddy, soaking wet and covered in burrs and, although remarkably fit little dogs usually fairly exhausted, their broad smiles indicated their satisfaction. They were undoubtedly very sporting animals by any standards and there was absolutely nothing wrong with their temperament. Their Chinese ancestors would have been proud of them, and rightly so. They loved life and lived it to the full. There was nothing wrong with their working ability or with their temperament, but it required a man of remarkable character and understanding to bring these qualities to the fore.

Temperament, however, can be a significant factor even when it comes to the actual mating itself. As any experienced breeder knows it can be a very simple business to mate a dog and a bitch on some occasions, while on others it is a nightmare process. The important thing is to choose the moment when the bitch is truly receptive. Sometimes this may be a very short period of time, sometimes on the other hand it may be several days or even weeks. Sometimes it is plain for all to see, and on occasions it is not at all obvious.

The presence of a dog on such occasions can be all revealing. The use of a small dog as a 'teaser' will usually make matters obvious enough. If the moment is right when the bitch is ready and the dog to be used is an experienced and willing sire the whole matter can be over quite quickly with no trauma whatsoever and a second mating a day later to ensure that success has been achieved should be almost a formality. There are, however, always bitches who are flighty or simply temperamentally skittish. There are others who for no obvious reason do not react in what may be simplistically termed the 'normal' way.

The important check is to note at once when the bitch first starts showing colour. The vulva, the external genitalia, will appear swollen and warm to the touch, hence the term 'in heat', and she will be licking the bloody discharge frequently. This will initially be a rich dark red, but towards the end it usually changes to a pale pink or brown. Theoretically she should then cease showing colour on the eleventh day when again theoretically, she should be receptive and eager to accept the mating. After a day's interval, if the timing has been right, she should, theoretically,. still be prepared and willing to accept the dog again. Be warned, however, that the period of showing colour may vary from as little as eight to as many as sixteen days between bitches of different breeds. This is a very variable factor.

In some cases, where the dog and bitch are together for several days they may of course couple several times. It is sometimes thus possible to mate a bitch deliberately three times with an interval of a day between each. Assuming they are only mated twice, however, the climactic mating should ensure that a litter is born around sixty-three days later. That at least is the theory, but, of course, in reality matters do not always go so smoothly and according to plan. Nor are any of these figures set in stone. Indeed some bitches barely show colour for more than a few days but are willing to accept a dog happily while others show colour for as much as three weeks and refuse any advances. Furthermore canine pregnancies have been known to last anything from fifty-seven to seventy days, although such extreme variations are very rare. There may be slight variations depending on different breeds, the age of the bitch, the number of couplings and other factors, but sixty-one to sixty-four days are the more or less accepted norm.

For the first few weeks at least after mating the bitch may be exercised as normal, although any chance of overstraining her is to be avoided as a matter of course. She is, it is to be hoped, a pregnant mother and undue strain is something to be avoided, even if she is ready and willing to work as normal. As the weeks pass and, hopefully, she begins to show signs of pregnancy it is always worth taking care but most bitches are capable of working pretty normally right up to the last week or two before the pups are born, by which time the pregnancy will probably have become fairly obvious.

There are always those who do not seem to realise that reasonable care of the bitch includes matters such as not expecting her to swim in freezing water to retrieve wildfowl in the last week or so of the pregnancy. I know one otherwise seemingly sensible dog owner who seemed quite surprised after allowing, indeed encouraging, his bitch to do just that when she subsequently aborted what promised to be a rather fine litter. Taking care of the bitch means avoiding undue strain throughout the pregnancy but particularly in those last few weeks, even if she is apparently showing no outward signs of imminent motherhood. Being a macho-man with a macho-dog attitude is all very well for Rottweiler dog owners who wish to flaunt the symbol of their manhood on the end of a lead, but it is not a suitable attitude for owners of pregnant bitches.

Yet, while undue exercise and strain should be avoided, over molly-coddling the bitch can be equally bad. Without sufficient regular exercise and with too much food the bitch is likely to grow excessively fat, which is not good for her and is not likely to help the whelping. Regular exercise and careful feeding with a good wholesome diet providing a sensible regime is all that is required. The feeding of extra vitamins and proteins, using additives such as bone meal, which are likely to produce more healthy pups with strong bones are, however, naturally worth while.

Because all bitches differ it is hard to say when the pups are likely to be obvious. It is, however, always possible to have the bitch scanned at around four weeks, and this will at least assure you that the bitch is pregnant and possibly give some idea of the number of pups, and sometimes even an indication of their sex, although it is not always guaranteed to be entirely accurate in either case. In practice, however, with many bitches you may see the pups moving and by placing a hand gently against the belly you may feel them kicking in the womb. In some bitches, however, it has to be said that there appear to be absolutely no signs of pregnancy at all even up to the last stages. Those are the cases where a scan can at least relieve the mind.

There are, of course, some other likely signs of imminent pregnancy to look for, such as the presence of milk in the teats. Although a likely sign of fairly imminent pregnancy the presence of milk in the teats, sometimes even leaking freely from them, is not always a sure sign that birth is imminent. False, or phantom, pregnancies are quite often seen in bitches that have had pups, and they may show every sign of imminent birth including teats brimming with milk. They may often start making beds and even try rather pathetically to nurse and feed a furry toy.

Sometimes such bitches have even been known to take on pups from another bitch and act as a surrogate mother. Knowing the whereabouts of such a possible surrogate mother, or a bitch who may have lost her pups for some reason and may be prepared to suckle the pups, is not a bad thing to have up your sleeve if there is a possibility of an extra large litter or if the mother turns out to have insufficient milk for one reason or another. It is, of course, seldom to be found when most required

In normal circumstances the signs that the bitch is in pup – the steady increase in girth, the movement of the pups themselves, then possibly the swelling of the teats and signs of milk present – should make it clear that the bitch is approaching the time when she is about to whelp. Eventually the weight of the pups will be seen to have moved significantly backwards towards the loins. When, however, the bitch finally loses any interest in food, the birth may be expected within around twelve hours.

The number of days she carries the pups is something that must, of course, vary with each bitch. Counting from the first mating it should be around sixty-three days, but sometimes it may be sixty-three days from the second mating, or she may not complete the full term and have them a day or so early, or even, perversely, a day or so late. As already mentioned there can be very wide variations. Nature does not always stick to a firm time schedule. On the other hand, if the pups have not appeared by the due date it is definitely advisable to have the prospective mother checked by a vet in case there are complications of some sort. In most cases, however, it will be found that the number of days has simply been miscalculated by the breeder. This is something that can happen very easily even in the best regulated circles.

With a bitch that is healthy and fit and is exercised normally each day there is really no reason why mating and pregnancy should not be a perfectly simple and straightforward process without any need for more than ordinary sensible care. This, of course, includes keeping an eye open for any unusual behaviour or symptoms. For instance, particularly where there are signs of bloody or discoloured discharge from the vulva, or when there is excessive urinating, diarrhoea, staring coat, hot nose or other similar signs of the bitch being off-colour, these are naturally cause for concern and possibly a visit to the vet. If there are any signs of sickness or illness it would be foolish to ignore them, but this should, of course, not be carried to excess. Running to the vet for every minor ailment is a waste of their time and your money.

For the novice breeder's peace of mind as much as anything else it is, however, probably worthwhile having the bitch checked over once or twice by the vet during the pregnancy. If it is decided to have a scan then a follow-up check prior to the date when the pups are expected is probably worthwhile. This will at least ease the prospective breeder's anxieties at this stage. The novice dog breeder of either sex is very like a male parent facing delivery of his first child and is often beset by needless fears and anxieties. In such cases the vet can usually be relied on to put matters in perspective.

Chapter 3 | THE MATING

Mating two dogs can be a very straightforward business with an experienced dog and bitch. If the bitch has reached around the eleventh day of showing colour and the colour of the discharge has changed from dark red to pale brown the time is almost certainly right. This can usually be checked by watching her reaction to having the area above her tail scratched. She should stand staunchly ready to receive the dog with her tail twisted sideways revealing ready access to the vulva. Little more should then be required than to leave the dog and bitch in an enclosed area, such as a

Teaser at work: Border terrier doing his best but too small to consummate _____

Dog mounting a willing bitch (Jackie Gibbs)

kennel yard, and let them get on with it. After a little prancing foreplay the experienced dog will approach the bitch, having investigated and licked her nether regions, and without further ado mount her, starting the mating process at once. The bitch herself, if fully receptive and ready for the mating, after probably a little playful response to his approaches will stand ready for him when he mounts her, simply twisting her tail, steadying herself and awaiting his entry. It can be as simple and straightforward as that, but it does not end there.

After the dog has entered the bitch's vagina and starts thrusting inwards the appropriately named bulbous glandis, the swelling at the back end of the penis, distends into a large spheroid shape and the two animals become locked together. This is known as the 'coital tie' and prevents them from separating after he has ejaculated his semen into her. They will usually remain locked together for a period which may vary from only ten or twenty minutes up to as much as an hour or even more. In such cases they will usually settle down resignedly after a short while. The dog will usually

Small dog and bitch being restrained after culmination of mating (Jackie Gibbs)

first remove his forelegs from the bitch, dismount and stand awkwardly at an angle then probably eventually get his hindleg over his still firmly locked-in penis so that they end up still joined together but back to back like a pair of bookends, patiently resigned, waiting for the muscular spasm to end and release them.

A coital tie may sometimes happen in humans when the vagina goes into a spasm and I am assured that a pin or similar sharp object jabbed into the buttocks will break the muscular spasm holding them together. I have however, never had any necessity to verify the truth of this. Should it be desired to separate the dogs urgently for any reason, if for instance the bitch is refusing to stop struggling or appears to be particularly distressed and cannot be easily restrained it might be worth trying this on the dog and for good measure the bitch as a last resort. Presumably this might have the effect of producing a countershock to their nervous system similar to that causing them to lock in the first place, thus allowing them to separate earlier. Be warned, however, that I cannot guarantee it will work and any interference with the natural mating process is usually inadvisable. It is worth emphasising that on no account should any attempt be made to pull the dogs apart at any time as this may result in serious injury to the dog and possibly the bitch as well.

If a nervous bitch is struggling unduly she is best just held firmly and soothed as far as possible to prevent her injuring the dog until the coital tie is over. As with much else to do with mating and dogs it is usually advisable to let Nature have her way as far as possible, simply restraining them and calming them down verbally and physically as far as possible if it becomes necessary to do so. If the handlers remain calm and show no signs of panic this is usually transmitted to the animals in any situation and they will normally react accordingly.

The novice breeder should be forewarned, however, that apart from this often tedious aftermath, the mating of dogs can be a very lengthy and difficult business at times. If the timing is wrong, as it very often is, and the bitch is not receptive in the first instance there may be a great deal of time-wasting foreplay with the dog approaching the bitch, licking her vulva then trying to mount her and the bitch rejecting him with a squeal but still making occasional playful approaches to him. This can sometimes go on for quite a long time especially with a young bitch and an inexperienced prospective sire.

An experienced dog will usually be able to force himself on a bitch if she is merely an inexperienced maiden bitch who is ready to mate but has never been covered before, or if she is almost ready and merely needing a modicum of firmness on his part. In such cases, however, care must be taken that the bitch does not try to pull away in near hysteria and possibly damage herself or the dog once they are locked together. It is always advisable to have an experienced restraining hand nearby ready to step in if necessary and calm the bitch at the critical point if required. In most cases this will not be needed but it is always best to keep a close eye on the proceedings and be ready to prevent any problems before they arise.

The presence of two handlers, one of whom at least should be experienced is undoubtedly preferable on such occasions. To expedite matters a dab of Vaseline into the vulva and then a guiding hand with the entry of the penis at the critical moment may well be decisive. This can be helpful even with an experienced sire. Outside interference may not be necessary but sometimes it is, and to avoid any problems it is best that the animals are watched and supervised as far as possible throughout the proceedings. One experienced handler is probably sufficient but two may sometimes be desirable in an emergency. If nothing else, two are at least company for each other to break what may be otherwise an extremely

Larger breed being restrained after mating (Tom Brechney)

boring and sometimes lengthy session where nothing in particular disturbs the boredom. Having something to read and keeping one eye on the dogs at the same time is not always easy.

There is always, however, an element of possible damage to either dog or bitch in any mating and it is therefore desirable to keep an eye open for any eventuality. At any stage when a bitch is in season, or even just coming into season, and a dog makes any advances it is always possible there may be some sort of quite unexpected problem arising as a result. While for the most part the worst to be expected is a growl or two and possibly some baring of teeth there can sometimes be much more serious consequences. It is always as well to keep a weather eye open for possible trouble.

I had a most unexpected object lesson in this on one occasion when a former bridesmaid and old friend of my mother-in-law's visited us. She was a statuesque figure, a one-time mezzo soprano, with a very considerable presence which had developed to such a degree over the years that in order to gather her Pekingese dog in her arms it was necessary for her to swing him on his lead and harness like a pendulum before catching him neatly when he had finally reached the required height and enveloping him in her more than ample bosom. Nero, as he was called, was rather a fine looking dog, although with somewhat unusually protuberant eyes even for a Pekingese. He survived this ignominious treatment with an air of resignation, possibly secure in the knowledge that it ensured him an ample supply of chocolate drops on which he was fed at far too frequent intervals for his own good.

At the time we had a fairly large gundog bitch in the room with us whom I knew was due to come into season shortly, but whom I thought was still of no particular interest to the opposite sex. Clearly our Chinese visitor thought otherwise and had more than chocolate drops on his mind. We had just sat down at a tea table laden with goodies provided by my wife when he decided that he scented possible carnal pleasures to be had and forgot the prospect of pieces of chocolate cake to come from his mistress As the object of his lust was lying down nearby and thus on a suitable level for him to do so he made a determined approach and tried to mount her.

She, like Queen Victoria in rather different circumstances, was clearly not amused at this unexpected approach from an oversexed furry pigmy and without changing her position snapped somewhat casually at him over her shoulder. We were most of us watching this byplay somewhat indulgently when, to my total horror and that of all the other spectators, the bitch's eye tooth must have accidentally caught him in the wrong spot for one of his protuberant eyes suddenly popped out of the eyeball and dangled from a couple of nerve strings or sinews on his cheek a full couple of inches below the gaping empty cavity in which it properly belonged. It was a totally unexpected and fairly appalling spectacle for all concerned, especially of course his owner, but also for me as owner of the bitch responsible.

I heard the long deep indrawn breath of a mezzo soprano beside me tuning up for a particularly prolonged and perfectly justified scream. Quite instinctively, without really thinking about it, I quickly bent down and scooped up the eyeball between two fingers and thumb and thrust it back into the socket. Very much to my surprise and probably everyone else's, it slipped easily back in place like a rubber ball squeezed into a hole. No scream ensued although there was a noticeable heaving of that remarkable bosom, and the Chinese gentleman himself had a somewhat surprised look on his face, which I am quite sure was mirrored on my own and everyone else's who was present as well.

As I recall it nobody actually commented on the event at the time, mainly I suspect because for some time we were all holding our breath and hoping the eye was not going to pop out again. Surprisingly it remained firmly in place and Nero himself was apparently none the worse for the experience. In fact he was soon happily guzzling his way through a sizeable slice of chocolate cake, which I surreptitiously slipped him beneath the table out of sheer relief. He also received his usual piece from his mistress and munched his way with gusto through that too, quite obviously blithely unaware of how close he had been to a change of name from Nero to Nelson.

As I learned on this occasion, however, in this most improbable fashion, when a bitch is in season it is always desirable to be careful when there are dogs around. In these circumstances almost anything can happen unless due care is exercised and injuries to either the dog or the bitch are always possible, sometimes even in the most unexpected ways. Those who favour muzzling bitches when they are first introduced to a dog may thus have a point, even though I do not personally feel it is likely to be necessary unless the bitch has an obvious vicious tendency. In such a case it is probably inadvisable to breed from her anyway. If in any doubt, however, it may be well worth taking precautions as this incident shows. If a bitch is showing a tendency to snap at the dog there can be no harm in fitting a light muzzle on her temporarily. A soft broad bandage secured around the muzzle may well suffice as a temporary expedient if a suitable muzzle is not readily available.

Maiden bitches, especially when not quite ready for the dog, can be very difficult to mate at times. A great deal depends on the nature and character of the bitch. Some are naturally flighty and flirtatious, apparently ready to play with the dog but refusing his advances whenever he gets serious. Others are dour and set in their refusal, snapping at the dog until they regard the moment as right. Either way they can be equally tiresome and cause endless time wasting and frustration for their owners. There are really very few things more boring than watching a dog and bitch sniffing each other endlessly and cocking a leg or squatting and clearly not intending to mate.

Once a bitch has been mated for the first time, however, they are usually ready enough to accept the dog a second time, but there can be exceptions where the bitch still proves difficult to mate even then. While on many occasions all is simplicity and nature takes its normal course there can be those maddening times when despite everything to all appearances seeming right the bitch proves adamant and the dog eventually loses interest. On such occasions the sensible thing to do is separate them and forget about the whole matter for a few hours, or even a day if that is possible, on the principle that distance, or time, makes the heart grow fonder. The danger, of course, is that the all important moment may be lost and it will then be too late for a further six months. It is this dire possibility which keeps many would-be breeders in a state of nervous anticipation when it is obvious to the dispassionate observer, who is not personally involved, that the bitch is simply not yet ready to mate.

I have known an occasion when a maiden bitch was being particularly

Several restraining hands for lurcher mating (Jackie Drakeford)

difficult and even an experienced dog had been repulsed where three strong men were eventually forced to intervene to ensure the mating finally took place. By the time that particular mating had been accomplished successfully most of those concerned, including the dog, were exhausted. The bitch, perversely, was looking rather satisfied with herself and ready for more, even though in human terms the proceedings would probably have been classified as aggravated rape of the worst order. It should be emphasised, however, that such occasions are, thankfully, fairly exceptional and most matings go more or less according to plan with individual variations depending on the animals concerned.

Even so canine matings do tend to be boringly lengthy by most animal's standards. Bullings are over in a very short space of time and stallions do not usually take very long, while couplings of deer or bison in the wild, for instance, are also usually fairly straightforward. There is even a certain grace and majesty in some matings. There is nothing about the mating of dogs, however, that can possibly inspire the onlooker to poetic fancies. The dogs themselves when locked together usually look faintly embarrassed and the reaction of most people on seeing them is either embarrassment or derision.

One particular occasion sticks firmly in my mind. I had been asked by a friend who owned an extremely handsome Great Dane if I would stand by and keep an eye on his dog's first mating with a bitch in case anything went wrong, as neither he nor the bitch's owner had any experience in the matter. We met, by arrangement, in the grounds of a large country house hotel where the owner of the bitch had been staying overnight and where a convention of some sort was taking place. She turned out to be a rather attractive young woman, in her early twenties, who was, however, very naïve and as inexperienced and nervous as her rather outstanding young bitch.

My friend was a thirty year old bachelor somewhat shy in his dealings with the opposite sex who had never met her before. Apart from having been put in touch with each other by the breeders of their own animals and speaking on the telephone to arrange the mating the two were strangers to each other. The mating itself, which, with a young novice dog and maiden bitch and utterly inexperienced owners, I had expected to be something of a nightmare, was instead completely simple and straightforward, if somewhat pachydermatous. After very few preliminaries and virtually no time-wasting skirmishing the two very large dogs were quickly locked together with the owners each holding a long chain leash attached to their respective animal and each blissfully unaware of the numerous possible traumas they had successfully avoided.

I had just advised them to keep hold of the leads in case the young dogs tried to pull apart, although they showed no signs of anything beyond blissful contentment, when I was called to the telephone and had to leave them to it. When I returned some time later I found them standing with their backs determinedly turned to each other, each still holding onto their lead and each puffing desperately at a cigarette, but neither of them saying a word to the other. They were both extremely red in the face and the dogs were still locked together, also back to back, while almost every single hotel window overlooking the scene was filled with appreciative male spectators who all seemed to be striving to outdo each other in offering bawdy comments and advice. It turned out that the convention, mainly consisting of commercial travellers, had been concluded unexpectedly early and alcohol had been flowing freely. Perhaps not surprisingly, the pair did not try to have a second mating after a day's interval, but the coupling still proved a great success in that a prize winning litter of pups resulted from it. I doubt, however, if either of the owners will ever forget it.

One sure way to avoid any such scenes is to arrange for the bitch to stay with the owner of the sire if this is possible. Even if they do not run a commercial kennels most owners of dogs advertised at stud are prepared to board a bitch over the mating period and this is a good way to ensure that the mating takes place with as little fuss as possible. Certainly the owner of the bitch is unlikely to hear if there have been any difficulties, as this might reflect on the owner of the sire. This ensures, however, that there is plenty of time for the dog and bitch to become acquainted as well as for the bitch to become truly receptive and ready for the mating. It is probably one of the best ways of ensuring a satisfactory mating. Having for a long time owned stud dogs myself, however, I know very well that even in such circumstances everything does not always go according to plan.

I recall with particular horror an undersized bitch, who looked distinctly like a cross-breed considering her size and general appearance, although the deceptively personable owner had shown me a copy of an impeccable pedigree when arranging the mating in advance. The bitch had been sent by train, arriving covered with fleas and lice and with a rather nasty kennel cough. She was supposed to be ten days into the season but refused to allow the dog near her. She was still showing colour and refused obstinately to show any inclination to accept the dog for the whole of the next week. She also showed all the signs of having been badly handled as well as severely neglected. In short she was a problem case who required fairly lengthy remedial treatment and reflected very badly on her owner. It was difficult not to feel sorry for her, but looking back on it, we should probably have refused to accept her and simply sent her back to her owner at once. That, however, is being wise after the event.

Dosed for lice and fleas, cleaned up, isolated and the kennel cough responding to treatment, but still showing some colour ten days later and due to be sent back in two days, the bitch was finally introduced successfully to the dog. She had to be held firmly on a slight upward slope to put her on the same level as the sire but, finally, after an unusually lengthy struggle involving everyone available, she at last accepted him. Only an hour or so prior to catching the train, she had a second successful mating before finally and with considerable relief we saw her on her way. Predictably we had an even greater struggle to extract the stud fee along with the cost of kennelling and vet's fees, finally having to resort to threats of legal action before extracting a very belated cheque.

That, however, was an unusually complicated mating with a difficult bitch owned by a particularly devious owner and probably sticks in my mind for that reason. If the stud dog is kept in a well run kennel sending the bitch to be mated there is almost certainly the best arrangement for all concerned. There is not likely to be any difficulty with the owners knowing whether the bitch will accept the dog or when it is the right time for the mating. The dog and the bitch can see each other every day and will, in theory at least, soon let all concerned know when the time is right. There will be experienced staff on hand who should know what they are doing and are able to cope with any problems that may arise. For the comparatively short time likely to be involved it may cost the owner of the bitch a substantial boarding fee and possibly a handling charge in addition to the stud fee but it will probably be considered well worth it in view of the time, trouble and anxiety the novice owner has been saved.

It is highly desirable to ensure that the bitch is in good health before sending her to the sire. Indeed some kennels demand proof that the bitch is free from any disease and is fit to mate before accepting her. The reverse, of course, should really hold good, as a dog may easily pass on diseases which may kill newly born puppies, such as herpes and fading puppy syndrome, to a bitch as well as vice versa, although fortunately both these examples are virtually under control in the UK. Many such infectious diseases can be picked up, however, wherever dogs are gathered together, as for instance at dog shows, hence occasional health checks are well worthwhile.

It is always a sensible precaution to have your bitch checked over by your vet before you send them to any kennel, whether for mating or for any other reason. If you neglect this precaution and the kennel to which you sent her claims she required de-lousing or the removal of other parasites or that she had any other health problems, more especially any infectious diseases, then, since you have no proof to the contrary, you must expect to have to pay for the privilege of having her 'cured' and accept the cost of any vets bills you may be sent.

This is only reasonable in the circumstances, if she was indeed suffering from any disease or infection when she left you, even if you were unaware of it. If the kennel can show you a veterinary report to prove it, then she has been endangering the general health of the kennels to which she has been sent and you must clearly be expected to pay any bills incurred by them for her care. If, however, you have a veterinary certificate to show that your bitch was in good health, clear of all diseases and fit to mate before she arrived at the kennel, that is hard to refute. It is in any event a sensible precaution to take since it covers you should the bitch catch any infection, such as kennel cough, while in their care.

If the dog lives close to the bitch it will be fairly simple to make sure that they are able to see each other during the crucial times. If they meet each other regularly from the time she is expected to come into season the rest should follow reasonably simply. They should have plenty of time to get to know each other and hopefully the dog's presence will expedite the bitch coming into season. In most cases the mating can then take place naturally and at the right time with very little fuss or bother. In most well managed matings when the timing is correct that is what happens.

It is only when the chosen dog is some distance from the bitch that timing difficulties can cause real problems, although difficulties may sometimes arise when the stud dog is serving other bitches as well. It is probably desirable that he does not try to serve more than three bitches in a week. Correct timing on both these counts can be fairly crucial. Driving any distance for a mating when the bitch refuses to take the dog can be a thoroughly tiresome business. It may mean spending several hours over each abortive mating as well as the time taken journeying backwards and forwards, and if the dog has recently served another bitch it may be further time wasted. In such circumstances it is probably more sensible to make do with another, possibly less desirable, sire, nearer to home. It is certainly a considerable incentive to make sure the bitch is absolutely ready to take the dog before she is introduced to him.

Of course one of the obvious ways of trying to ensure the bitch is receptive and ready for the dog before making a long journey is to try her out with a dog near her home. The availability of a neutered dog at this time, as has been noted, is a useful adjunct. While this is probably a good test it is by no means a certainty. As well as the question of the timing of the season, which in some bitches can linger on for a surprisingly long time, and in others end quite suddenly and abruptly, there can also sometimes be an element of personal preference involved. A dog, or a bitch may for some reason simply not like the prospective mate.

Mating any animals can be a very tricky process. I once watched with interest an experienced stud groom try for over half an hour to induce a thoroughbred stallion to cover a very handsome looking thoroughbred mare. The prospective sire would have none of her as he was quite clearly enamoured of a small pony mare who had been brought into the stable yard to mate with him and had caught his eye as she was being led past him. He trumpeted his desires at once in no small measure. Until he had served her he would not look at the thoroughbred mare, who was paraded fruitlessly before him without him showing the slightest interest in her. He made his priorities very plain and the good looking thoroughbred mare had to wait until he had had his way with the rather scrubby looking pony. After that, in rather a bored fashion, having made it abundantly clear that he would only perform his accepted function as and when he wished, he duly covered the mare he had previously refused to service.

The same sort of preferences may sometimes arise with a bitch who is enamoured of a local mongrel dog but will not look at the pure bred sire by whom she is supposed to be mated. Usually keeping her with the chosen sire at the appropriate time will overcome such difficulties, but sexual preferences between animals can sometimes become quite ridiculous. On one absurd occasion I had to pursue a large bitch of mine who had become totally enamoured of a visiting Jack Russell which lived fairly close at hand. He was, I have to admit, a rather delightful cocky little dog who had been visiting us at my request, as we had no stud dog at the time, to check whether she was in season. Rather tiresomely she had obviously decided that he was the perfect sire of her dreams.

She ardently reciprocated his advances and followed him and his owner down the road as he departed. She adamantly refused to leave his side, still flirting skittishly with him and apparently totally unconscious of their totally absurd disparity in size. She was obviously very put out when I put her on the lead and led her back home, while his owner informed me that her diminutive suitor, who was clearly quite as enamoured of her as she was of him, howled his laments lugubriously all through the night.

Despite such minor problems the principle of using a local dog, preferably perhaps one that is neutered, as a sounding board, or 'teaser,' to see if the bitch is truly ready to mate is generally a sound one if it is necessary to take the bitch some distance to a sire. When a bitch is really ready to mate, as noted, scratching her at the base of the tail will usually cause her to switch her tail firmly to one side or the other and hold it there with her vulva protruding ready for the dog. Introduction to a dog at this stage is usually merely a formality. In such circumstances even a novice dog should have no difficulty in completing the mating successfully.

The whole process can indeed be a very simple matter on most occasions, especially when the bitch is showing such clear signs of being ready and willing to mate. The attentive reader will have realised, however, that very little to do with mating or whelping bitches is as straightforward as might be expected. Difficulties can sometimes arise in the least expected ways even when all the indications are favourable.

Even where the bitch is ready, apparently fully receptive and eager, and the dog is willing and experienced there can still be difficulties. As has already been indicated, when the dog is much larger than the bitch or vice versa there can sometimes be problems. My late mother-in-law, for whom I had a great admiration, was a keen breeder of St Bernards for many years, initially using outside sires on her bitches, although latterly using her own.

However, for a regrettable and unforgettable period the only dog she kept was a very sporting and determined Pekingese. Whenever the bitches were in season that poor little dog became the most determined and ardent lover it is possible to imagine. Despite his best efforts, fortunately, he never consummated a mating, although on one occasion he was caught leaping from the stairs, launching himself in a desperate do-or-die effort like a small self-propelled rocket, ending up with a resounding thump on the floor after bouncing off his intended target.

In practice, if there is a noticeable disparity in size between the dog and bitch, that Pekingese had the right idea. It is sometimes necessary to place a small bitch on a slight slope, or on a raised platform such as a flat box or covered platten, so that the difference in size is less noticeable and she is better placed for the dog. The same principle works as well in reverse if the bitch is larger and the dog approaches her from above so that he is well placed to mount her without any problems. In practice, however, unless there is a total and insurmountable disparity in size, as with the Pekingese and the St Bernards, or say a Jack Russell and a lurcher, Nature will usually find a way.

There is, however, as has already been indicated, a certain amount to be said for keeping a small sporting dog, such as a Jack Russell, along with bitches of a larger breed as a 'sounding board', or barometer of when they are coming into season. Like the Pekingese with the St Bernards kept by my late mother-in-law, there is unlikely to be a misalliance. The poor chap, even if neutered, may, however, well be desperate for some weeks and if he is vocal his howls of thwarted passion can be a distinct disadvantage. You may even have to resort to ear plugs or send him away for a while, but whether you are thinking of breeding or not, he will as a matter of course provide a useful indicator of when the time is ripe. He will also as a matter of course probably forget his house training completely and 'leave his mark' around the place. There are both advantages and disadvantages to this form of barometer, or 'sounding board', which can sometimes be leaky as well as noisy.

All this may sound as if mating dogs is a minefield, and in some cases this can indeed be true. There can be disadvantages and difficulties and on occasions they may even seem extremely daunting, especially to any novice breeders experiencing their first mating. In the main, however, it is a natural process and the dogs themselves are usually the best guides. In the majority of cases it can be more or less left to them but it should be emphasised that is always advisable to keep a close eye on the proceedings. In the case of maiden bitches especially it is always desirable to have some experienced supervision on hand. Leaving too much to chance or Mother Nature is not always advisable, and those who do have only themselves to blame if matters do not work out as they had hoped.

The basic calculation that a bitch should be ready for the dog after showing colour for eleven days is all very well in theory, of course, but bitches may vary very considerably not only between breeds but from bitch to bitch. There will be some bitches who hardly show colour at all and are very hard to catch at the right receptive moment. There are other bitches who continue to show colour for as much as a fortnight or more. There are yet other bitches who are clearly ready for the dog from the earliest moment of showing colour. There are still other, exceptional, bitches who seem ready to take the dog and mate at any period from long before the very first signs of the vulva swelling to long after colour has ceased.

There was one very good working bitch I had who broke a hindleg very badly while leaping an old drystone dyke which gave way under her. I rushed her to the vet, who X-rayed her and kept her for nearly a week before returning her with the leg encased in plaster. He mentioned in passing that he thought she might be showing signs of coming into season shortly and that if this was the case it would be advisable not to mate her as this might tend to hinder the healing process.

While I agreed with him entirely, keeping her away from any contact with our stud dog after her return, it was clear she must have had other ideas beforehand as the day the plaster finally came off she had a litter of eight strong healthy pups. She had clearly mated successfully before the trauma of her accident and her stay at the vets, although never at any time showing any obvious signs of being in season even after returning from the vet and, of course, she had no second mating. She had been at the time, however, running freely during the day with our stud dog and there can be no doubt that they must have coupled unseen and with no sign of eagerness on his part or impending season on her part. Although in fact it all worked out very successfully without her recovery being in any way impeded, and with the bonus of a very fine litter of pups, this was a good example to me of how important it is to watch each bitch with great care during the run up to the likely period of her season.

There are indeed exceptions to every rule. It is up to the prospective breeder to watch the bitch carefully and work out as far as possible in advance what her particular propensities seem to be and, accordingly, how best to prepare for the mating. It cannot be repeated too often that in the vast majority of cases all will go smoothly and according to plan. The average bitch usually comes into season in the normal way and most matings go very smoothly within the normal parameters. There are, however, always exceptions and various possible difficulties which may be encountered. It is often when least expected that things can go wildly wrong.

Asking experienced advice at any stage when you are not sure what to do or something seems to be going wrong is merely common sense. From checking on the bitch's seasons to finding a suitable sire there are always knowledgeable people willing to help. Everyone except those few fortunate enough to be brought up in experienced dog owning families has to start from scratch. If in doubt never be afraid to ask for help from your vet or from an experienced breeder. It is better by far to be safe than sorry at the expense of an animal who is necessarily putting its trust in you.

Chapter 4 | CARE OF THE PREGNANT BITCH

Once the mating has been successfully completed and the bitch may be presumed to be satisfactorily impregnated, as has already been pointed out, there is no need to start treating her as if she was suddenly made of fragile crystal. The normal feeding and exercise routines may be continued as usual. If she is working hard there is no particular reason to ease off for the moment: her normal standard of work may be continued for several weeks. Certain minor additions to her feed may, however, be usefully made. A small amount of bone meal, protein and vitamins regularly added to her feed can do no harm and may well result in healthier and stronger pups, but the main thing is to ensure that her feeding is regular and nutritious. In the normal course of things with a well ordered kennel of dogs or a regular feeding schedule for a single bitch this should mean little or no alteration in her usual diet.

A great deal, of course depends on the bitch herself. A sturdy healthy bitch naturally will tend to thrive to some extent regardless of how she is treated. There is an old saying that some dogs will survive and even thrive on a diet of no more than potato peelings, and to judge by the diets on which some dogs are fed this is not far short of the mark. A diet of raw tripe hung from a hook which the dog has access to at any time is not really good enough, but in the past this was quite a common means of feeding, supplemented only by water, and it is still not unknown in some areas.

By contrast the shepherd who fed his collie dogs almost entirely on porridge, which again was quite common at one time, was probably doing quite well by them. With the addition of an occasional dead ewe found on the hill they probably did extremely well, but then his job to a large extent depended on them working effectively. As he may often have had no other company for weeks on end they probably in many cases shared the same food as well as having a deep bond of understanding in their work. There is no doubt that even on these monotonous and fairly primitive diets bitches thrived surprisingly well and produced healthy litters of pups.

Furthermore, they were probably worked right up to the time of whelping with little or no respite.

Given that a sturdy healthy bitch really requires very little attention out of the ordinary it can still do no harm to look after her and try to prevent accidents, as well as trying also to improve her diet even in small ways and thus her chances of producing a good healthy litter of pups. Her diet, for a start, does not need to be as monotonous or uninspired as potato peelings, tripe or porridge. It does not need a master chef to add a little variety to a dog's diet and today there are countless varieties of biscuit and whole feed on the market as well as tinned dog food at very reasonable prices. Some of course are extremely expensive, and by no means as nutritious as they are advertised to be.

To judge by some of the feed scandals that have been uncovered in recent years, some of the pet feeds on the market were indeed far from desirable or nutritious. Some of them at least appeared to consist of meat condemned for human consumption which to ensure it is not sold as such it is then sprayed with blue dye. All of this is presumably then removed by high powered hoses and possibly chemicals before it is finally cut up and cooked. After thus being duly 'processed' and then canned, high-powered advertising may then sell what is only one step away from fertiliser as 'specially prepared and highly nutritious' pet food 'of the finest quality'. Fortunately the majority of pet food on the market, whether canned meat or made up in biscuit form, is comparatively good, even if not necessarily as wholesome as much of the advertising makes it out to be. There is a vast variety of sound and genuinely nutritious pet food to choose from and there is no excuse for not seeing that the bitch is adequately fed.

There is no need to err too far in the other direction, however, and a diet of chicken and smoked salmon or similar delicacies is uncalled for even if affordable. The normal sensible balanced diet which a working bitch should receive in the usual way of things will do perfectly well with the addition, as noted of a few proteins and vitamins likely to help the growing pups and if nothing else give the breeder the feeling they are improving their prospects.

The bitch, if fed a reasonably good balanced diet, and exercised regularly, will almost certainly manage perfectly well. It is important, however, especially if the weather is warm, to ensure that she has a good supply of fresh water always available should she require it. A regular half pint or so of milk can also do no harm. I have known dogs belonging to dairy farmers who had almost unlimited milk available along with the occasional egg from free-range hens and their coats shone like silk. Both milk and an egg now and then are undoubtedly useful additions to the diet of the pregnant bitch.

If you are fortunate like us you may have a very good local butcher who can provide you with remarkably cheap but very good quality dog mince. We are able to feed this either raw or cooked along with a mixer biscuit and occasional tasty additions such as fish and vegetables. We are also fortunate in living close to the sea and a harbour which still has some fishing boats occasionally allowed out to sea. When the boats return with any sort of a catch on board undersized fish and fish trimmings, which make very good animal food, can usually be bought extremely cheaply or are even sometimes given away for the asking. This too provides a source of healthy food for any bitch in whelp.

Most butchers and fishmongers, however, have similar useful animal feed available, which is available cheaply or would often otherwise quite possibly have to be thrown away. As a touch of variety and a good source of protein these are well worth adding to the normal feed of the pregnant bitch. They need not add much to the normal feed bill and may be regarded as a sound investment in producing healthy pups.

If you are not lucky enough to have access to similar sources of fresh nutritious feed, then your local supermarket may be worth approaching. It is often the case that large superstores have to dispose of food which is about to reach its sell-by date and are prepared to let it go free, or at very low cost, to pensioners or sometimes for animal feed. I was once even able to feed our dogs for some time on a diet of smoked salmon and pâté obtained in this way. Mostly it is, however, rather more mundane, but then fish such as haddock or cod caught by fishermen from the sea, even if a little smelly, may well be more nutritious than similarly smelly farmed smoked salmon.

Nutrition, however, is a subject which the experts will always find something to quarrel about, whatever the sources of the food. For instance I know of at least one breeder who has a regular arrangement to obtain left-overs from a chef in a large hotel. He occasionally obtains some very exotic doggy fodder in return for a little game in season and occasional rabbits and pigeons. This, however, seems to me to be verging on the old arrangement of collecting pig-swill, which is now rightly illegal as likely to spread disease. While there may no longer be the hazard of finding cigarette ends or cigar stubs amongst such waste fodder there may still be bottle tops or broken glass and similar hazardous substances to be found in feed from such a source. Wherever your dog food may be obtained from there is however, no excuse for not providing a reasonable and healthy variety of feeding for your pregnant bitch and it need not be very costly if you look for sources such as these suggested.

As in any pregnancy it is, of course, important to keep a close eye on the calendar. Around the half way mark, about the fifth week or so, it is probably advisable to start easing off a heavy workload slightly and keeping a rather closer eye on the bitch. By this time she should be beginning to show some visible signs of pregnancy, but regular exercise is still desirable. As well as a sound diet a regular regime of work or exercise is still needed. Without being kept in physical shape there is no point in keeping her suitably fed. The two go together and the bitch needs regular work to keep her fit and well muscled. To ease up on her normal exercise simply because she is carrying pups is doing her no favours. Keeping her well muscled and in good condition is the sensible approach. Allowing her to get unduly fat and out of condition is downright stupid. A regular routine of sensible feeding and controlled exercise combined is more important now than at any other time.

If it is desired, from about the fourth week it is possible to have the bitch scanned by the vet to ensure that she is in pup and thus possibly obtain some idea of the size of the litter. This is very simply done at no risk to the bitch and should not be very expensive. It is not possible to learn the sex of the pups by this means but to confirm that she is in pup at this stage and know roughly how large a litter, if not the exact number, it is likely to be, when there are no other positive signs, is a major plus point for modern technology. Another plus point is that there is positively no risk to the bitch or pups involved in the process.

In fact, by this time some bitches are already showing the early signs of pregnancy with very slight swelling detectable and even in some cases signs of the pups kicking in the abdomen. There is said to be what is termed 'a window of opportunity' about the third to fourth week when by feeling the bitch gently the pups may be felt moving. It is also said that this ability to feel the pups passes within a few days and it is not then possible to feel the pups moving again for some weeks. I have not personally found this 'window' to be thus limited, but it may be so with some breeds and not with others. It is usually possible to feel faint signs of movement in most bitches from quite an early stage around the third or fourth week and from then on right through the pregnancy, although no doubt different bitches will vary in this as in much else.

Certainly these signs are usually able to be felt and even seen clearly enough by the sixth or seventh week, when the maiden bitch especially may sometimes be seen peering down at her abdomen in a slightly puzzled way as the pups start kicking quite vigorously. On the other hand there are always those exceptional bitches who show no signs whatever of being in pup right up to the last moment. In cases such as these there is no doubt that a scan can be very helpful and will at least relieve the breeder of the

Bitch pointing and showing the weight of the puppies not yet fully back (Michael Brander)

nagging worry that the mating has been unsuccessful and that all his or her efforts in arranging the mating, having the bitch covered and then feeding her up and looking after her have been in vain.

Assuming that a scan has been taken and proved the bitch in whelp the breeder has at least one less problem to worry about. The probability is that in the normal course of events the various tell-tale signs, the swelling of the belly, the slight but noticeable enlargement of the teats, the faint but already perceptible movement of the pups to which the bitch herself may inadvertently have drawn attention by sometimes casting a questioning

The same bitch on the day of whelping and showing the weight fully back.
(Michael Brander)

glance at an unexpected twitch from that source, would have allowed the knowledgeable breeder to come to the same conclusion. Even so, to have the certain confirmation of the pregnancy by 'the wonders of modern science' is bound to be a relief. From this stage onwards at least the breeder knows that if all goes well they can expect the arrival of a litter of pups.

Now is the time, if the breeder has not done so already, to start spreading the word far and wide of the successful mating and looking for suitable homes for the pups. If their breeding is from sound working stock on both sides there should always be homes for them, but the sooner the word is passed around the more likely the prospective buyers are to come forward. The quicker the word gets round in suitable circles the better. There are, it must be remembered, plenty of other breeders, many of them with pups that they will claim to be every bit as well bred as those you hope your bitch will produce in due course. Failure to take every opportunity to sell pups in advance can result in them not being sold beforehand and the breeder instead being left with several puppies aged ten or twelve weeks eating their heads off and sometimes having to be sold or even given away at a substantial loss.

If the breeder personally does not have enough contacts in his or her immediate circle of acquaintances the owner of the sire should be willing to spread the word that pups of the mating are available. In addition the breed club itself will almost certainly be ready to help If the breed club secretary is notified of the mating. An advertisement in the breed club magazine may also be helpful and usually does not cost a great deal. More expensive but sometimes very well worthwhile may be an advertisement in the local newspaper or specialist sporting press. It may also be worthwhile advertising on the Internet. This is an increasingly common way of advertising specialised products such as puppies, and reaches a wide, if sometimes questionable, market.

It is really important, indeed absolutely essential, to be prepared to use every means available to advertise the likely arrival of the pups well in advance. It should be a matter of the highest priority to have homes available for them all before they even arrive. Otherwise you may be left with only six weeks or so to sell ten or more puppies. Thereafter there is always the dire possibility of being left with a litter of unsold fast growing youngsters at the half way stage between attractive saleable puppies and untrained, or only semi-trained, near adults, eating enormous quantities of food and needing hours spent each day for both exercise and training, Even the finest of litters when seen at that awkward unattractive gangling teenage stage are more difficult to sell and frequently difficult even to give away. That is when the novice breeder who has not had the forethought to sell his or her puppies in advance questions their sanity in even considering breeding.

Before he or she even contemplates breeding from the bitch, however, it is usually possible to form some idea of the likely size of the litter. The number of teats the bitch has, for a start, should at least indicate how many pups she can feed comfortably, although by no means a guarantee of how many she will have. The size of the litter from which she herself came may give some idea of how fertile her dam was, if no more. The size of the bitch, of course, in itself will give some idea of how many pups she is likely to have. In general a small working bitch such as a terrier is by all the laws of probability going to have fewer pups than a larger breed such as a Labrador or lurcher, but, of course, much may depend on factors such as whether the mating was entirely successful, how many times the bitch was covered, and so on. In the end, however, almost any bitch can spring all sorts of surprises when it comes to the actual whelping, from having only one puppy to having double figures, or even simply a phantom pregnancy.

Whether the bitch has been scanned to check for pregnancy or not it is still worthwhile checking the bitch over daily as a matter of course. This daily check up is always desirable for any dog, simply to ensure general health and fitness, but in the case of a whelping bitch it should be a little more thorough. Eyes, nose, coat, feet, rear end and vulva should be checked briefly for general health and the latter for signs of any discharge, while teats and abdomen should also be examined.

Anything unusual such as hard swellings in the teats or abdomen, painful reactions to touch, wax, swelling or signs of milk in the teats should be noted. Anything potentially serious, such as signs of discharge or bleeding, staring coat, dull eyes, lack of colour in the gums, or obvious distress, will usually be quite plain to see, and fortunately it has to be said is very rarely encountered, but may well be grounds for a visit to the vet for a check.

If the bitch should have any unusual problem, such as being involved in a dog fight and being seriously bitten or mauled, being hit by a car or involved in a car accident, or otherwise suffering stress and trauma, it is not necessarily the end of the pregnancy. It is surprising how much stress an in-whelp bitch can survive without losing the pups. In any such case, however, it is of course advisable to get her to the vet for a check over as soon as possible.

If the bitch has suffered a broken limb or other serious injury, and depending what stage the pregnancy has reached, the vet might recommend aborting the litter in the bitch's best interests. On the other hand if the injury is not life threatening and can be healed comparatively easily the vet may simply treat the bitch and recommend extra care with the birth. Fortunately this is not a decision which has to be made often, but when it comes down to basics the life of the bitch should be paramount and even if it is necessary to abort the litter she will normally be able to breed again at a later date.

Should the bitch suffer a minor injury such as a damaged toe, or contract a minor malady such as eczema, it may involve problems with the ordinary course of the pregnancy. In the former case she might be unable to exercise in the normal way, in which case there is a danger of her getting too fat unless care is taken to curtail the quantity of her feed a little and increase the nutritional value to compensate. In the latter case it would be desirable to clear it up as quickly as possible before the pups arrive because it might easily be passed on to them, and such infectious diseases can cause significant problems in young pups. These are the sort of things that a daily check should spot before it becomes serious enough to cause trouble. If the novice breeder does not trust his or her own abilities to spot incipient problems of this kind they may prefer to have a more knowledgeable friend help them out or bite on the bullet and accept the cost of a veterinary visit if they feel there may be anything seriously amiss.

There is always the problem that if the bitch becomes ill, especially by picking up some infectious disease, it may not be possible to dose her with the normal cures since this might have adverse effects on the pups. Fortunately bitches in pup are usually particularly healthy. It is important, however, especially in the early stages to make sure the vets know that she is in whelp whenever they are dosing her for even minor ailments. A great many modern medicines are unsuitable for mothers-to-be and can cause problems. This is a hazard which could very easily arise if the vet is not kept informed of the bitch's condition.

There are other quite common problems which it is also highly desirable to ensure the bitch is free from, although, theoretically, in properly run kennels they should not be present. The bitch should, of course, be free from worms and fleas, lice, ticks or any other such surprisingly common infestations. Any of these may, however, arise at times even in the best run establishments and it is surprising how an infestation of one or other may suddenly occur.

As the bitch moves into the latter half of her pregnancy it is probably best to treat each one as an individual case, as indeed they are, for no two are entirely similar and it would be very boring if they were. The temperament of the bitch is the all important guide. A strong determined bitch will probably very happily continue working as normal almost to the very last minute even when heavily pregnant. It is, of course, desirable even in such cases to ease off a little and ensure that she does not work too hard however willing she may be. In fact it is probably more important to see that a really keen bitch of this type does not overdo it than to keep an eye on the bitch with a sunny easy-going temperament that does not bestir herself very readily.

Towards the end of the pregnancy it is also important to see that the less energetic type of bitch, which is anyway prone to put on flesh, does not become too fat. This type of happy-go-lucky rather idle type of bitch should be exercised carefully and regularly to ensure that she does not put on too much weight. The aim is to reach the final stages of the pregnancy with a bitch in good physical condition and ready to cope with the stresses and strains of giving birth. Regular exercise is an essential part of the programme for any whelping bitch, whether they are keen on it or otherwise. It is, however, the exception rather than the rule that will not readily go out for a walk, even if they may set their own pace or begin to flag towards the end.

It is always, however, a moot point what different people consider 'reasonable' exercise. I have known people regularly cycle at speed with the dog running behind or even exercise the dog while it is running behind their car, apparently incapable of appreciating that their dog cannot readily keep up the same pace as their machine. I even knew one case of a man who took his young puppy of three months running half marathons and wondered why it developed a heart condition. Everything is relative and common sense must be exercised. It is always wiser to err on the side of caution rather than overdo matters with a pregnant bitch.

During the last fortnight or so of the pregnancy the signs of approaching motherhood should be beginning to show fairly clearly. It is important by then, if it has not already been done, to introduce her to the whelping area where she is to have her pups. With the birth by now fairly imminent, the sooner she is accustomed to it the better. If the bitch has been scanned or the pups have been felt moving at least you can rule out the possibility of a phantom pregnancy and know that a litter should be forthcoming. It is wise, however, as the old saying goes, never to count your chickens before they have been hatched. There are always unfortunately, those rare exceptions when even at this stage everything goes horribly wrong.

I had a sad example of this when writing this book. Some old friends of ours were staying with us along with their very well trained young golden retriever who was due to pup in three weeks. In fact I had arranged to be present at the birth to take photographs to use as illustrations for this book. She left us with her owners and seemed in very good health until a week before the pups were due, when she started showing signs of discharge and bleeding at around two in the afternoon. By eight that evening she had to be put down having lost the pups due to a fortunately fairly rare condition known as thrombocytopenia.

This particular problem can also affect humans though not usually fatally. It is caused by a fairly rare condition causing a low blood platelet count, known as immune-mediated thrombocytopenia, or IMT. The blood platelets assist the blood to clot normally and a very low platelet count may mean that any bleeding may cause severe haemorrhaging. The result is that when bleeding is triggered internally, as in this case by the pressure of pups on the placenta, the blood clotting system fails to operate and nothing can be done to stop the loss of blood.

Fortunately such problems are extremely rare, although haemorrhaging in this way might also be caused by a bitch scavenging around and swallowing warfarin laid down for rats. There are also a number of possibly infectious causes for a bitch aborting towards the end of the pregnancy. If the worst should happen care should always be taken in such circumstances, because as well as infecting other dogs or cats some of these infections, such as brucellosis, may possibly be passed on to humans. It is advisable in any such case, if possible, to bag the foetuses and any afterbirth for examination, but in these circumstances, where the cause of the deaths is still unknown, care should always be taken to avoid any skin contact in case of infectious disease. Disposable rubber gloves should be worn if these circumstances arise.

For the same reason, of course, it is desirable to disinfect very thoroughly the whole area involved and remove all traces of blood and mucus or other matter remaining on the scene. Until veterinary checks have been made it is also advisable to keep the bitch in isolation and nurse her with care. As in any such circumstances a vet will probably already have been called in to assist, they will be able to take control of the post mortem on the litter and check the health and condition of the bitch. They will also naturally ensure that due precautions are taken. It is as well, however, to be aware that in any such unfortunate circumstances while the cause of the abortion is unknown there is always a possibility, however remote, of infection passing to other animals or humans and hence considerable care should be taken.

In normal circumstances, as the pregnancy draws to a close there will be no such dire complications and the signs of a healthy impending birth are usually obvious enough. The teats are usually prominent and initially somewhat waxy, but when the birth is fairly imminent they are likely to become distended with milk and indeed may be showing drops of milk at times. The pups by this time should be readily seen moving and the bitch may quite possibly be almost barrel shaped and moving heavily. On the other hand in some cases there may be virtually nothing obvious to show the bitch is in pup. Where they are obvious, however, there will usually be a noticeable shifting of their weight towards the rear as the time for the birth approaches.

When the bitch shows no interest in food it is usually a sign that the birth will probably be within the next twelve hours. Further signs of approaching whelping are when the bitch starts making beds and moving

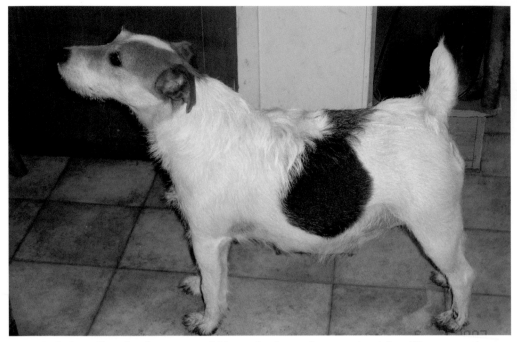

Jack Russell terrier due to pup within twelve hours, but pups' weight still not moved back to loins (Colin Harrison)

around restlessly as if searching for somewhere to lie down. Such uncharacteristic behaviour is fairly typical of a bitch who knows instinctively that whelping is imminent and in the manner of the wild is looking for a safe and suitable shelter in which to have her pups.

At this point just prior to the whelping, but with its approach imminent, most bitches will also begin to show some signs of agitation, but here again temperaments vary immensely. Some bitches will begin to get very fussed and agitated, finding it difficult to remain still. Others will calmly lie down and prepare to get on with proceedings as if it was nothing out of the ordinary. Most, however, will be somewhat fussed, showing signs of animation and probably continually licking at their vulva. When the foetal sac appears and the waters burst with a gushing of liquid then the birth has finally started.

Chapter 5 | PREPARATIONS FOR WHELPING

In the vast majority of cases the normal pregnancy takes its course and with the minimum of fuss the pregnant bitch reaches her due term and settles down to produce her puppies as Nature intended. Even if matters run their course in this way, as in general they do, there are certain simple ways in which the bitch can be helped. With a minimum of advance preparations the bitch can still be assisted by her owner and the actual birth made a lot easier both for her and her pups.

For a start, it is always advisable to decide well in advance where the whelping should take place. Anyone who has whelped bitches regularly should naturally have a special area set aside for the purpose and will presumably be well prepared, simply following a well-tried and well-rehearsed routine. They are, however, in the nature of things unlikely to be reading this book. For the novice breeder it is necessary to prepare both themselves and the bitch for the coming event and there are a considerable number of ways in which matters can be made easier both for the bitch and for the owner as well as the pups themselves.

It is desirable fairly early on to choose somewhere for the whelping where the bitch will feel at home and is comfortable, which is also reasonably secure and protected from outside interference. A roomy whelping bed or basket in a reasonably secure and preferably undisturbed secluded environment to which she is accustomed is the aim. If this can be in a secure kennel or room separate from any other dogs or outside distractions with plenty of space around it for the owner and any assistants to be present this is ideal. However, when it comes down to it, like many human births if they occur unexpectedly, the whelping can at a pinch take place almost anywhere. Many whelpings do take place, be it intentionally or otherwise, in the surroundings where the bitch normally sleeps, whether that is a kennel outside or a basket in the house. It is advisable therefore to ensure either that this area is suitable for the whelping or that she has been accustomed for some time to sleeping in the new surroundings where it is intended that the whelping should take place.

Greyhound close to whelping but weight of pups still well forward (Jackie Drakeford)

If it is decided that the normal sleeping area is not really suitable for whelping it is advisable to move the bitch to the chosen whelping area some time in advance so that she can become thoroughly accustomed to it. It is desirable that she feels completely at home and secure there. The surroundings should be draught free, quiet and secure from any interruptions. Ready access to a self-contained outside area is also desirable if possible. The whelping box itself can be readily constructed of hardboard or plywood. It should ideally be roomy enough for her to be able to lie down comfortably at full length and move around easily if necessary. It should be built with reasonably high sides to keep her free from draughts, with a suitable easy entrance made for her if desired.

For bedding, which will quickly become wet, bloody or otherwise soiled and need replacing, there are several options. Many people use old newspapers which can be used flat or cut and crumpled. They tend to be quite effective but messy and sticky and the pups can become covered with pieces sticking to them. I prefer a bed with a waterproof cover and over that a thick towelling cover with elastic fittings at the corners holding it tightly in place. This in turn can be covered with other thick towels, which can be

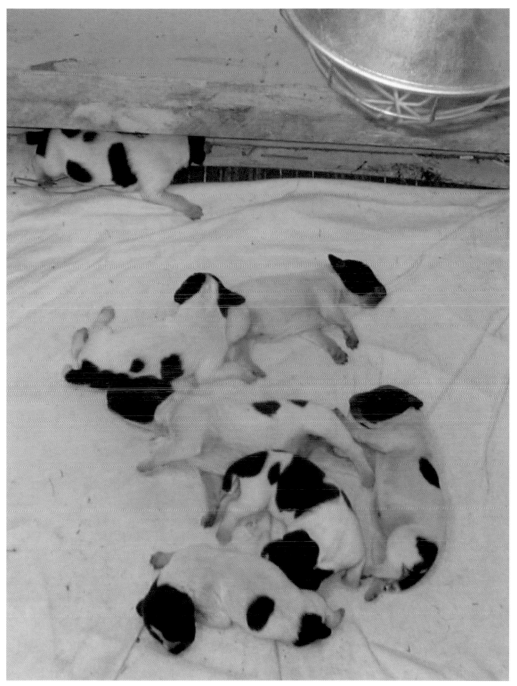

Pups in whelping pen on towelling base with venturesome pup under creep safe from being overlaid when dam returns (Tom Brechney)

Large oval whelping basket with tube creep hung from metal hangers (may also be secured by tape and blocks). Fitted waterproof base. Towelling cover used for whelping

easily replaced as necessary, as can the one fitted with elastic over the bed. They can then be washed, dried and used again as required.

It is also desirable to have a box ready with a blanket-covered hot water bottle, or some similar means of heating for it, such as a heat lamp. This should be at hand waiting for the pups when they start arriving and should be placed close to the whelping bed while the bitch is having the pups. After each pup has been born, been dried off and been introduced to a teat and had its initial intake of milk they can then be placed out of the way in the warm box when the bitch starts her contractions in the throes of producing the next. There they should settle quite happily until the whelping is over.

In addition to the box for the pups, it is necessary to have a further supply of good absorbent rough towelling ready for the whelping. It is also desirable to have a good sharp pair of blunt-ended scissors and a bottle of iodine with a plentiful supply of cotton wool swabs on hand ready for use when required. These may be used to cut the umbilical cord and apply a dab of iodine to the severed end on each pup as soon as it has been separated from the afterbirth and has been thoroughly dried in the

Dam and pups in whelping pen with creep all suckling happily under lamp on towelling
(Tom Brechney)

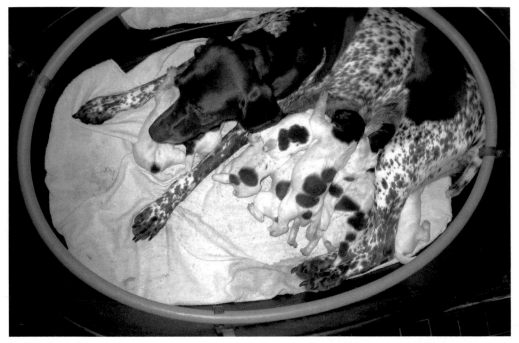

Thick hosepipe and thin metal strips bent in a vice serve as hangers held in place by light metal bolts bored through plastic side to act as oval creep.

towelling. There are those who advocate simply snapping the umbilical cord between the hands, but unless care is taken this may inadvertently cause a rupture. In addition it is useful to have a fairly small clean plastic syringe on hand to clean the noses and mouths of the pups of any mucus. Some people also like to have some woollen or cotton thread ready to tie off the umbilical cord, to avoid any possibility of infection if the end is left open. Finally there should be a set of scales handy in which each pup can be weighed in turn and, where there are no distinguishing markings, numbered with an indelible pen for subsequent identification.

A creep is also a useful addition to the whelping box. The idea is commonly used with sows having a litter of piglets, and the same principle holds good with pups to prevent them being crushed. This is a comparatively simple construction. It consists of a square or rectangle of two-by-four wood lathes the exact shape of the whelping box and fitting snugly inside it. It should be held by supports about four inches above the base of the box depending on the size of the dam and the likely size of the pups. The principle is that when the bitch lies down she is less likely to accidentally overlie a pup which has struggled round behind her, as there is then room for it to survive. It should, however, only be necessary for the first three days or so because after that the pups are usually strong enough to survive without it. By this stage it may even sometimes become more of a hazard than a protection. As soon as it has served its purpose and the pups are strong enough to survive without its protection it should be removed.

If wooden lathes are used for the creep they can if desired be padded for further protection with towelling. As the creep is simply slotted into the whelping box and is supported by wedges it can readily be removed and cleaned if it becomes smeared with blood or mucus. The design, like the whelping box itself, can have considerable variations. Rubber or plastic piping may be used instead of wood, which, having round edges, can be an advantage, especially if hung inside a semi-circular plastic whelping basket. Any handyman should be able to construct a creep fairly easily which sits snugly inside the whelping box and is readily removable when required. In the same way, a whelping box to suit the bitch's size is easily constructed of hardboard or plywood.

I use a simple box design cut in half with a semi-circular entrance for the bitch in one side which can be readily blocked up if required to keep the pups inside, or draughts at bay. The bottom half makes an excellent whelping box indoors, and the two joined together make a useful covered box which can be used in an outside kennel, if necessary, to protect the pups from any draughts and acclimatise them gradually when, or if, they are moved to outside kennelling for the first time. When they are accustomed to the great world outside the top can be removed to harden them off and later used as a second box for them as they grow larger if required.

A window on one wall of the whelping area is useful to allow a view of the bitch and pups without disturbing them. Alternatively, a microphone attached to the whelping kennel should be enough to warn the owner when there is a problem during the night in the first crucial days if a pup is in distress and in danger of being overlain. Nowadays CCTV cameras can also be installed comparatively cheaply and are another useful means of supervision without disturbance. Because it is desirable to avoid too bright a light when the pups are newly born and for the first week or ten days while their eyes remain closed, it is also important to make sure that, while there is plenty of light for the actual whelping, the area where the pups will be sleeping is not exposed to over-strong light.

In the week before the whelping is due it is desirable to start checking that everything is suitably prepared and ready. This, of course includes the bitch herself. By this stage she should be showing the various incipient signs of expectant motherhood. She will probably be growing visibly larger. Her teats may be more prominent, and, in a bitch who has had pups, may even be already showing milk. In long haired breeds she may well be showing signs of shedding hair around the teats another sign of approaching birth. If there are no signs of this happening it is probably advisable to trim the hair to allow the pups easy access.

The main thing is to have all the preparations for the whelping ready and finalised at least a week, but preferably nearer two, before the date the pups are due, and to have the bitch thoroughly settled in by then. The longer the bitch can be accustomed to the surroundings where she is going to whelp the easier it will be for her. Clearly if she is ushered into completely new surroundings in which she is not entirely at home she will not be as comfortable and relaxed as she will be when in a bed to which she is thoroughly accustomed and where she knows she is secure.

All the accoutrements which are likely to be involved, scissors, cotton wool, towels, iodine, plastic syringe, thread and rubber gloves, if they are to be used, should all be handled in her presence by the whelping bed so that again she is not put off by the sight of anything strange when whelping time arrives. The box to which the pups will be removed for safety and kept warm while the whelping is in progress should also be present, if discreetly in the background. In practice, when the time comes she will almost certainly be too concerned with the actual whelping and the arrival of her pups to pay too much attention to what is going on around her, but it is just as well to try to ensure that she is not distracted by anything strange.

For instance, the effect of someone she does not know arriving at the whelping can be quite surprising at times and is very much better avoided if possible. Even the mildest-mannered dam can suddenly become extremely protective of her offspring when she has a new litter to protect. It is not just the presence of strangers that can trigger such reactions, either. Even the arrival of someone whom she knows quite well can very easily cause similar unexpectedly fierce reactions. For bitches who associate the vet with unpleasant experiences, such as injections or painful operations, their arrival may also sometimes cause just such an adverse reaction, especially when they start to handle the puppies. This is something to look out for and be prepared for in advance.

The protective motherly instinct is sometimes very strong indeed and more than enough to turn what may be a normally shy and retiring bitch quite suddenly into a raging beast baring her teeth and intent on protecting her young against attack. In smaller breeds such as terriers and spaniels this may not be a particular cause for concern but with larger dogs such as greyhounds or lurchers it may be another matter altogether. Yet bitches that might have been expected to behave fiercely in such circumstances may be

GSP bitch almost due to whelp in whelping pen and subsequently required Caesarean
(Tom Brechney)

surprisingly quiet. It is always difficult to know how they will react and it is as well to be ready in every way and to make things as easy as possible for the bitch by preparing the surroundings and accustoming her to them well in advance as well as keeping the number of people present at the whelping to a minimum.

When a bitch is in a secluded area where she already feels at home and secure she is naturally much less likely to react in a hostile way to anyone approaching her. If, however, she is in an area to which she is not fully accustomed, where she feels insecure, she is likely to feel she has to react in a more challenging way to protect herself and her pups. This is a perfectly understandable reaction, and if the bitch is moved to her new quarters well in advance it can probably be avoided altogether, although some bitches will, initially at least, react to the advent of pups by being highly protective.

It is always desirable in any event that the whelping kennel should have reasonably easy access to an open space such as a kennel yard. If this is the case there may be no need to move the mother and pups to an outside kennel as they grow larger, as the whelping area can double for an outside kennel for the pups. This is in fact a very convenient arrangement if the kennelling can be planned in this way. It may not always be desirable in a professional kennels but for any amateur it is probably more convenient than having to move the pups as they grow older.

Another advantage of having the whelping kennel with easy access to an outside space is that it is sometimes desirable to let the bitch have a little exercise between delivery of the puppies, especially if a pup seems to be causing her to strain unduly. It may be that it is a breech delivery or a particularly large pup which is making matters difficult for her. In such cases a brief walk round may help to ease matters by repositioning the puppy and preparing the bitch for another series of contractions. In any event some bitches seem to like a short walk about between pups and the opportunity to get outside for a moment or two during their whelping. In that it may settle the next pup in a more suitable position for whelping it is probably a very good thing. Whatever the prospective mother seems to desire at this stage is probably a good thing within reason. If she demands a brief walk about this is almost certainly going to do no harm.

It should also be unnecessary to add that a bowl of clean water for the bitch to drink if she feels thirsty should always be on hand. During the actual whelpings it is unlikely that she will want a drink, but between pups, after straining at length, she may like to have a few laps and it is always as well to have it present. After the whelping she is very likely to be thirsty and in fact can become considerably dehydrated, but at that stage it is probably as well to let her have something warm and nutritious such as broth or a warm milk drink at first, although a bowl of water should still always be available.

A whelping kennel that is indoors, but with ready access to an open yard and with an interior window allowing easy viewing of anything going on inside without the bitch being disturbed is undoubtedly the ideal arrangement. With a basin providing hot and cold water and air conditioning, or at least a means of heating if required, there is not much lacking. If a microphone or CCTV camera is installed picking up all the sounds of the pups and mother when she starts whelping or once they are whelped, the owner can retire secure in the knowledge that if there are any crises in the night they are likely to be easily overheard. If the owner is sleeping close at hand it is then possible to check on what is happening without even having to enter the kennel.

This may all sound rather excessive, but it is in fact merely following the methods used by many sheep farmers and shepherds who are lambing possibly four to eight hundred ewes or more each year with multiple births now the rule rather than the exception. Over the years they have had time to refine the business of dealing with small animals giving birth to the ultimate degree. With such a large number of births to deal with they are likely to be up for nights on end and have over the centuries refined their methods so that they can obtain the maximum amount of rest possible and at the same time be on hand and able to oversee matters at a moment's notice.

There is nothing to be lost by copying some of their better ideas, and in fact a great deal of benefit to be gained. Why be uncomfortable, and why not look after your animals to the best of your ability at the same time? Sheep farmers have got the business of attending to small animals giving birth down to a fine art over the years. Modern sheep farmers are accustomed to using all the very latest technology available to solve their problems, and it would be foolish not to take advantage of their expertise and the methods they have developed when they can be of assistance.

The average dog owner whelping a bitch for the first time may not be able to aspire to such perfection, or even want to do so. However it should be possible to adapt a number of these ideas and provide something like a good whelping space for the bitch. If there is a ground floor spare room with access to the garden, or an enclosed outdoor space, that is a start. Many cupboards in kitchens with access to the garden have probably been adapted by amateur breeders over the years to provide a suitable whelping space for the bitch in an emergency. Most of the other suggestions can usually be adapted to the surroundings to a greater or lesser degree to achieve the greatest benefit possible for the bitch and at the same time the maximum convenience for her owner.

While it is desirable to look after the mother-to-be as far as possible it has also to be remembered that countless bitches have whelped naturally without any assistance over the centuries. There is every likelihood that even if everything failed and you were called out to some emergency so that you were unavoidably away at the time your bitch whelped she would survive the whelping perfectly well and have the pups by herself without any help from anyone. Nevertheless, you will naturally want to do the best you can by your bitch and helping to deliver the pups is an experience no owner should miss, quite apart from the fact that you may be able to help if any problems should arise, and naturally would wish to do so.

It is, however, very important not to get too worked up about the whelping yourself. Amateur breeders, especially at their first whelping, can understandably enough very easily become quite emotional and involved. Remember, however, that your feelings can always readily be communicated to your dog. While not being too laid back it is equally important not to become too intense or too worried should the situation seem to become a little tense at times. Becoming too emotionally involved is not going to help your bitch if she is in difficulties, and if she senses that her owner is upset in any way this is likely to have an adverse effect on her.

Even if it is the first whelping you have attended, and even if the bitch is your first dog and the apple of your eye, it is important to keep a sense of proportion and remain calm. Once the waters have burst and the bitch starts the actual whelping it is essential to remain as detached as possible. To become too worked up and anxious is the worst thing you can do as inevitably your own sense of worry and insecurity will be conveyed to the bitch and unsettle her.

Keeping a sense of proportion and remaining calm is absolutely essential throughout the whelping, even if you may feel that things are not going well. If you think that you may need the assistance of an experienced friend there is absolutely no harm in asking for help. Any experienced dog owner who has whelped a bitch or two will usually be happy to assist and it is only sensible to ask someone for help if you feel you may need it. Advice is all very well, but having someone experienced on hand is even better.

If you do feel in need of help it is probably best to start from the moment you decide to mate your bitch. An experienced guiding hand is always worth having and no one will think any less of you for asking for help and assistance at any time. In due course you may be able to help someone else in similar circumstances. As with most matters concerning dogs, of course, one of the best guides in the whole business will ultimately be the bitch herself. Even a maiden bitch usually knows instinctively what is required and in the majority of cases will be the best arbiter of what she needs.

The inexperienced dog owner will usually do well enough if he or she pays attention to the obvious requirements of the bitch and is guided by her actions and simply does his or her best for her. After all, giving birth is one of the most natural functions there is, and animals of all kinds have been procreating perfectly naturally for millennia without assistance. In the majority of cases all goes well, but having an experienced advisor on hand is always helpful just the same, if only to soothe the fevered brow of the novice breeder.

Chapter 6 | THE WHELPING

As noted earlier, it is important to note the dates of the successful couplings as accurately as possible, because the birth should take place approximately sixty-three days afterwards. This is of course not a hard and fast rule and if there have been two or even three couplings then the sixty-three days may be counted from the first, but that may for some reason not have taken properly, and the second mating may prove to be the significant date when the mating was properly consummated. In either case it is desirable to watch the bitch very carefully from around the sixtieth day, and from the sixty-second day to keep watching for signs of imminent whelping. If there are no signs of whelping by the sixty-third day after the second mating, assuming there were two, it is probably desirable to check with the vet and have the bitch examined.

If the bitch has been scanned and has proved to be in pup then by the sixty-third day after the final mating the pups should be imminent. If she has not been scanned there is always the possibility that it has all been a false alarm and that she has never been in pup but is showing all the classic signs of a phantom pregnancy. In the former case the pups may be due at any moment, or there may be problems in the offing. It may well be desirable at this stage to call in the services of the vet for an examination in case there could possibly be problems. In any event, if only to relieve the uncertainty it is probably a good thing to do so and if there is a problem it can hopefully be solved at once.

There is a school of thought which recommends that the bitch's temperature is taken daily for a matter of ten days before the pups are due. When the temperature drops a point the pups should then be due within twelve hours. If they do not appear on schedule it is suggested that the vet should be called as there may be problems. This is all very well, and may indeed be an accurate way of assessing the bitch's progress, but bitches do tend to vary individually quite apart from differences between breeds. It is also always possible that something other than the pregnancy might affect the bitch's temperature. To my mind any novice breeder would do well to

Plummer terrier due to whelp at any moment with weight moved back
(Sue Rothwell)

forget anything to do with temperature as it could do little more than cause their own to rise.

There are usually other more visible signs which provide as good a warning of imminent birth. Generally the bitch will start to lose her appetite about twenty-four hours before whelping, and will not look even at normally tempting delicacies for a matter of up to twelve hours before the birth. This seems to me as good a general sign as could be wished. If by then the weight of the pups has also moved visibly backwards towards the loins and pelvic canal yet she still has not shown signs of whelping then it might be time to start thinking about calling the vet.

If the waters have burst and the bitch is straining really hard for half an hour or more after that, then it is certainly time to call the vet. If you cannot get veterinary assistance within a further half hour and you have been able to get her to move around to no avail, it may even be advisable as a last resort to disinfect your hands and insert two fingers very gently into the bitch's vulva, soothing her all the while as much as possible. If you can feel the pup and grasp hold of any part it may be worth pulling very gently to help the delivery. If the protective envelope around it has burst the chances are that the pup may be already dead. Immediate action is all that is likely to save it. In these circumstances, if she cannot be helped immediately, the

Terrier whelping with pup's nose showing
(Sue Rothwell)

bitch may well need a Caesarean. Except in an emergency of this kind, however, any such action on the part of a novice breeder would be highly inadvisable.

In normal circumstances, if the bitch fails to pup when thought to be due the most likely probability is that she is perfectly all right and there has merely been an accidental miscounting of the dates on your part or the bitch is just slightly overdue. By the end of the sixty-third day it is, however, probably advisable to call in the vet. He, or she may be able to expedite matters with an injection if they feel it is desirable, or at least indicate that all is well. If, sadly, it has been a phantom pregnancy and the bitch has not been in pup at all, while showing all the signs of it, at least the bitch may be served again and hopefully will produce pups the second time round. It would be as well, however, to have her checked over in case there is some internal abnormality to explain why she failed to conceive.

In the normal course of events, however, the signs of an imminent whelping are usually fairly plain to see. Assuming that the bitch has been scanned or is very obviously pregnant, as the whelping time approaches closely, apart from her obvious disinterest in food, the weight of the pups can usually be seen to have moved significantly backwards towards the loins. As well as losing her appetite she will probably start moving around uneasily and her teats may also already be showing little drops of milk. She may start trying to dig up her bed to make a nest. She may also start panting at intervals, possibly squatting as if to urinate, and finally a small grey gleaming sac, like a small balloon filled with water, pops out of the vulva. When the water sac, or bag, bursts and a rush of clear fluid drenches the towelling this signals the advent of the placenta and the imminent arrival of the first pup. The contractions will probably start at this stage, further signs of imminent whelping, and very shortly the first pup should appear.

It may be, however, that the bitch shows only a few of the signs mentioned, or indeed, none of them. There are always those bitches which seemingly refuse to conform to any of the rules. There is little that can be done in such cases except to watch them carefully as the time approaches and hope for some of the signs to manifest themselves, as some almost certainly will, even if not as obviously as in more normal whelpings.

I have known a bitch that did, admittedly, show some signs of whelping though not particularly imminent and, by my reckoning at least a day early, demanding to go outside for an apparent call of nature. Once outside she squatted and appeared to be urinating normally, but it must have been the waters bursting as she promptly dropped two pups in quick succession in the snow in the kennel run before it was even apparent that they were coming. It was fortunate that I was keeping an eye on her and saw what

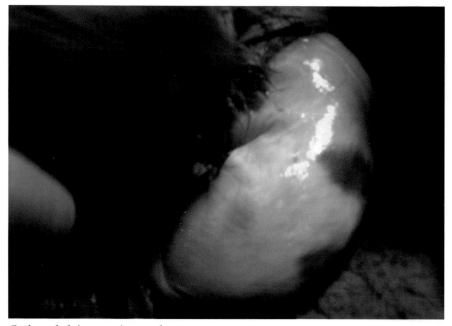

Cocker whelping pup in membrane (Jackie Gibbs)

was happening by the light of a torch. I promptly rescued the pups and returned them and the mother to the whelping kennel. Those pups and the rest of the litter, I am happy to say, all survived and arrived without any trouble, but it was a somewhat unexpected start. Be warned, however, that the prospective mother can always take you by surprise even if you are both watchful and expecting the arrival of the pups at any moment. It is advisable to be ready for anything and hope thus to avoid being taken by surprise.

Assuming that the whelping takes a more normal course the bitch will usually settle happily enough in the surroundings chosen for the event, more especially if she has been accustomed to them for some time beforehand as suggested. It is desirable, however, to have certain preparations made in advance. As noted already a good supply of clean rough absorbent towelling is always a first essential. This will end up thoroughly soiled and bloodstained but can be washed and re-used if so desired. A good pair of scissors and a supply of iodine are also essential to have on hand along with a plentiful supply of cotton wool swabs to apply the iodine as and when required. A clean plastic syringe is also useful to clean out the pups' nostrils and mouth if they are blocked with mucus.

The whelping bed itself should be covered with a good absorbent

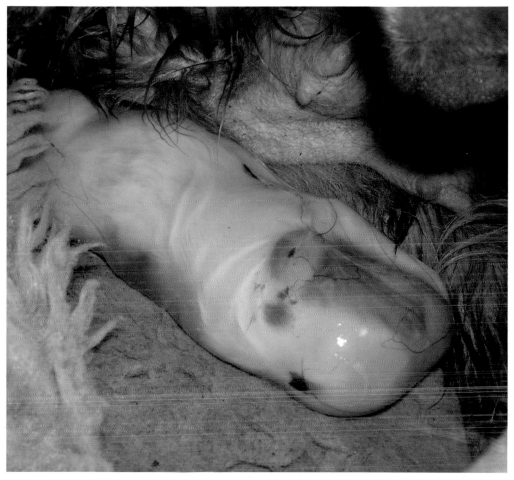

Pup delivered but still enveloped in membrane (Jackie Gibbs) ————————

towelling secured in place by elastic straps on top of a waterproof cover. As soon as the waters burst, hopefully signalling the imminent arrival of the first pup, the towelling will probably be fairly comprehensively soaked. The bitch will probably be licking herself frantically and also doing her best to lick up most of the liquid. As soon as it can be done without interfering too much with the whelping it is probably desirable to cover the wet bedding with fresh dry towelling or to replace it if possible. Following the bursting of the waters, however, the bitch's contractions and the imminent arrival of the first puppy will probably interrupt matters. Hopefully, first its nose and then its head, enveloped in the mucous membrane envelope in which it

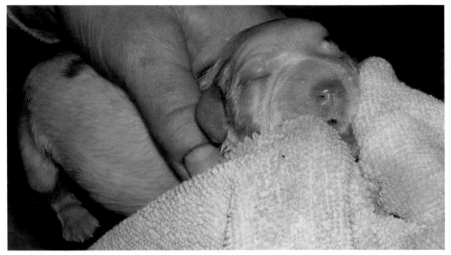

Clearing pup's mouth and nostrils to ensure breathing (Jackie Gibbs) ─────────

has survived in the womb, accompanied by a greeny black mess of afterbirth, will start to appear. Naturally this will become the focus of attention for bitch and owner.

The first pup will hopefully arrive in a normal manner and it is probable that the rest that follow in due course will mirror its arrival. The bitch will be seen to be straining convulsively and ideally the nose of the first puppy will appear protruding from the bitch's vulva enveloped in the birth membrane. After a further contraction or two the entire head should appear and then as she strains convulsively yet again the shoulders should follow with a rush, and then the entire puppy enveloped in the slippery membrane will slide into view with the umbilical cord still attached and the afterbirth following, all being abruptly deposited on the surface of the whelping basket. The bitch will probably immediately and instinctively start eating the afterbirth and membrane and sever and eat the umbilical cord.

In a natural birth, by herself, she would probably then lick the puppy vigorously and when it was dry and squalling loudly snuggle it close where it would naturally home in on a milky teat and start suckling. Acting as midwife, the whelping assistant should pick up the pup as soon as it has slipped free of the bitch, when it is still limp and covered in mucous membrane. They should remove the envelope of mucous membrane, leaving that for the bitch to consume along with the afterbirth. It is then desirable to snip the umbilical cord with the scissors even if it has already been severed by the bitch, leaving around an inch or so, and dabbing this with cotton wool soaked in iodine.

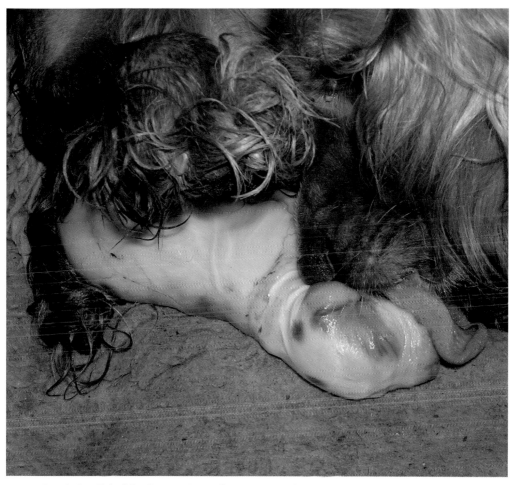

Pup being licked by dam and membrane removed (Jackie Gibbs)

Meanwhile the pup will often seem quite limp and lifeless, showing no signs of breathing. It has only five or six minutes to emerge from the mucous covering and start breathing before it either dies or is brain damaged. Left to herself in the normal course of events the bitch, having consumed the afterbirth and bitten through the umbilical cord would roll the pup around, licking it energetically until it is dry and breathing. In lieu of this it should be rubbed quite briskly for a few moments in a piece of rough towelling until it is more or less dry and starts giving tongue and eventually is squalling loudly. If required the syringe may be carefully applied to suck away any mucus blocking the mouth, nose or eyes. Then, if desired, after being thoroughly dabbed with iodine the inch or so remnant

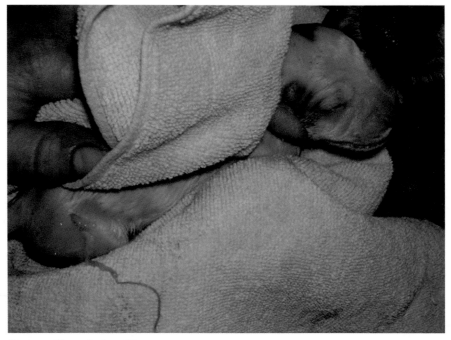

Drying off pup in towelling (Jackie Gibbs)

of the umbilical cord can be tied with thread to prevent any possibility of infection. It will then duly wither and fall off in a day or so.

After the pup has been vigorously dried in the rough towelling, as indicated, it should start showing signs of life, at first giving tongue and then finally squalling loudly. Then after it has received the dab of iodine on its inch or so of umbilical cord and been briefly examined all over for any obvious defects such as serious deformities, open hernias or ruptures, it may be introduced to the mother. During this time she will probably have been too busy eating the afterbirth to pay much attention to what has been going on. She should, however, by now have finished her cleaning up operations and will probably by this time be anxious to see her pup.

She will probably then lick it, often surprisingly roughly, rolling it around the bed in the process, as she would have done in the normal course of events after eating the afterbirth. This is usually a perfectly straightforward business, but, especially with a maiden bitch, there is sometimes a danger that after instinctively eating the afterbirth, when she is then introduced to the first pup she may become confused, especially, perhaps, if the pup has not been very effectively dried. Instead of licking it, she may then start biting it by mistake and may even injure it. This is also a possibility when

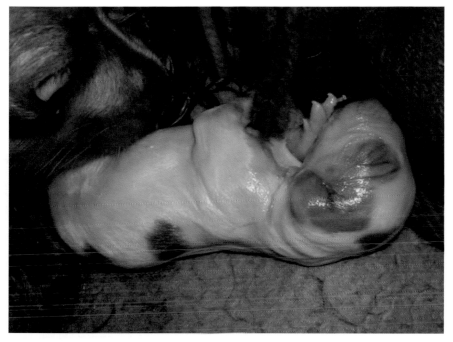

Pup being rolled round roughly by dam (Jackie Gibbs) ———————————

a highly strung maiden bitch is whelping by herself for the first time and is a good reason for overseeing the birth. It could, however, be the fault of the whelping assistant in introducing the pup to her as she is still eating the afterbirth, and due care should be taken to make sure this does not happen. With later pups any such problem is less likely, but care should still be taken with a maiden bitch at all times when whelping.

If there is any sign of the bitch possibly being over rough with the pup then she should be restrained and introduced to it with caution. Normally there is no problem and the mother may be left to attend to it by herself for a few minutes, probably rolling it over and licking it vigorously to dry it further before lying down and curling herself round it. The pup may then, however, be given some further assistance by introducing it to a teat and it should be seen to be fastening firmly on to the teat and suckling freely before finally leaving them together. The milk obtained from the teats immediately at birth is called colosterum, and is filled with antibodies vital to the pup's future growth and well being. It is important that, as far as possible, every pup has its share and care should be taken to try to ensure this.

The bitch will probably immediately snuggle down with the newly

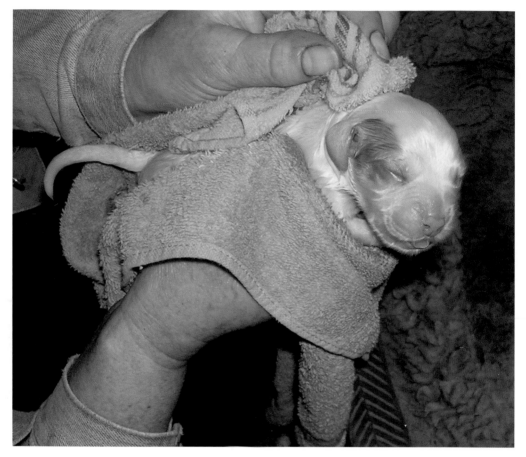

Partly dried off, breathing and giving tongue (Jackie Gibbs)

whelped pup allowing it to suckle happily. She should then be left alone to allow it to do so and to nurse it before the next set of contractions starts. When these become pronounced, announcing the imminent arrival of the next pup, it is time to consider removing the first pup. As soon as it is felt desirable to do so it may be removed to safety and placed in the already prepared artificially heated puppy basket where, after its initial sampling of its mother's milk, it should settle down quite happily. In due course the next pup, after being safely delivered, dried off and having its umbilical cord attended to in the same way as the first, may then take its place on a teat and for a short while have its turn receiving the mother's full attention.

This time there should be no danger of her mistaking the pup for the afterbirth and damaging it in any way, but if she has shown any signs of

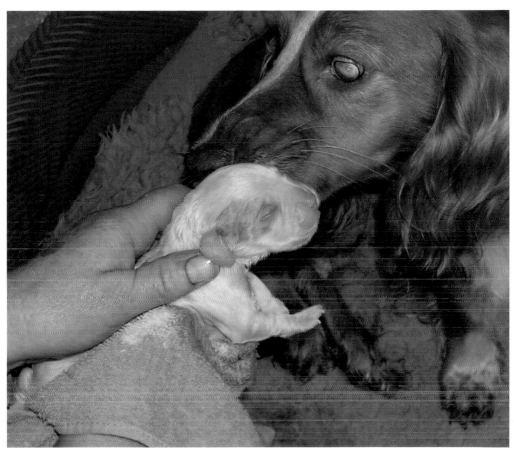

Being introduced to the dam after she has dealt with afterbirth (Jackie Gibbs) ————

nervousness with the first pup due care should be taken when introducing each new pup to her for the first time and while settling it in with her. There is always a possible problem with a nervous or highly strung young maiden bitch and a close eye should be kept on her to see that no pups are accidentally damaged. When the contractions start again each pup can then be moved on in turn to join its siblings in the puppy basket while a further pup comes into the world and joins the litter. Hopefully this routine will continue steadily without any problems until the final pup arrives and the litter is complete.

The dam's reactions to the birth of the first puppy will usually give an immediate idea of how she is going to behave from then onwards. Most maiden bitches are fairly excited and somewhat worried by the events, but

Umbilical cord still attached to dam and ready to be cut (Jackie Gibbs)

they should naturally start to eat the afterbirth, and if given the membrane and remains of the umbilical cord will be fairly involved with that while you are dealing with the pup. Then when you have dealt with the pup and it is giving tongue she will probably start looking for it anxiously and can be introduced to it safely, although, as indicated, special care should be taken with the first arrival.

The bitch will probably in the normal course of events roll it over and over, licking it roughly and finally snuggling down round it so that it can get at the teats. Then is the best time to introduce it to a teat and calm her down at the same time. Soothing words and calming patting will not come amiss at any time, especially if she seems to be unduly worried or is refusing to settle. The human voice can always have a calming influence but perhaps especially during whelping. The knowledge that you are on hand to help during this naturally somewhat traumatic time is obviously a help and comfort to the bitch and it does no harm to keep talking to her and encouraging her whenever she appears to require reassurance.

The bitch should then be allowed time to settle down and recover from the excitement of the first delivery in preparation for the next arrival. Suckling the new arrival usually has a calming effect in itself. Although sometimes one pup may be followed almost immediately by another, there is usually a gap between pups which may be anything from a few minutes up to a half an hour or even as much as an hour.

Time variations between different breeds can, however, be considerable and some breeds may take a rest between one batch of pups and another of a couple of hours or more. Especially where there have been three couplings, and pups may have been conceived as much as four days apart, there may be a very protracted pause between one batch of pups and another. Normally, however, any period longer than an hour may mean there is a problem, such as a breech delivery. A short walk around may be helpful, but any lengthier period with the bitch continuously straining may give cause for concern.

Assuming the next contractions start normally, however, when the bitch starts moving around restlessly it is probably desirable to remove the pup that is suckling and place it in the prepared puppy box with a warm piece of towelling securely covering a hot water bottle, or with other means of heat such as a heat lamp. While the bitch is in the throes of giving birth, especially in the case of a maiden bitch, it is always possible that she might inadvertently damage or even overlay a pup if it is left in the whelping area with her.

On the other hand it is always desirable, in the intervals between the births, to leave at least one pup with her so that she can nurse it normally and feel the customary maternal reactions. If they are all removed she may stop straining and not unnaturally be more concerned about the whereabouts of the pups she has already whelped, more especially if they are not warm enough and are giving tongue. If they are warm, quiet and contented, all huddled together in a heap, and she is feeding at least one, this should keep her quite happy without having too many around her to concern her and leave her free to get on with the business of producing the next puppy.

The intervals between the pups will vary with each bitch, of course, and indeed may well vary considerably between various breeds, but ideally about a quarter of an hour to half a hour is what might be expected. A breech delivery, i.e. with the hindlegs foremost rather than the normal head first delivery, can sometimes be difficult and may prove awkward for the bitch. An extra large puppy may also prove a difficult task, and for a maiden bitch sometimes proves a sizeable obstacle, especially if the pup's head should get turned backwards, although sometimes the shoulders can also prove a major problem with an extra large puppy. In such cases the bitch may be seen to be straining hard and may get up and move around. Sometimes an awkward presentation of this kind can be helped by manipulation. It is, it should be stressed, generally not advisable to try to interfere manually unless you know what you are doing and in such cases when the bitch has been straining for some time to no apparent effect it is probably best to call in the vet to assist.

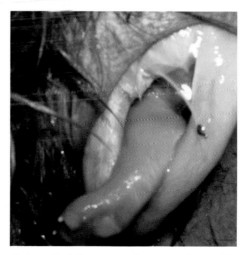

A breech delivery starting to arrive safely
(Jackie Gibbs) ─────────

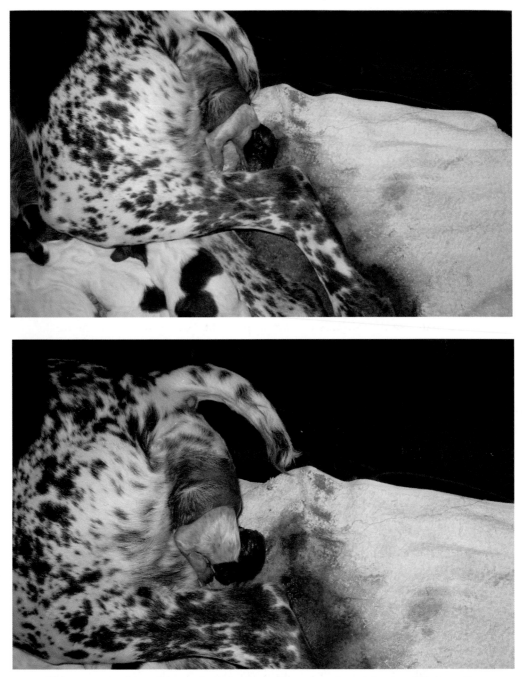

This sequence shows the puppies being born. The puppy is arriving head first – notice the bitch's greatly distended vulva. The puppy's large head has caused the mucous membrane to disintegrate and the contents are on the towel. (Michael Brander)

In cases such as these, however, where there is a difficult presentation, or a particularly large pup, walking the bitch around is usually well worthwhile trying in the first place. It may allow the pup to become repositioned, and this is usually all to the good because it may then be placed more favourably for the birth. This may result in the pup appearing shortly afterwards. Occasionally a badly positioned pup may even be delivered while the bitch is standing up or moving around.

Sometimes a maiden bitch, especially, may have a very considerable problem with a large pup or a breech delivery. Walking her around may allow the pup to become better positioned, or the contractions may increase and the pup may arrive, but may tear the vagina or the vulva slightly in the process. In these circumstances the bitch will somewhat naturally usually react with a shrill yelp or screech of pain and if the tear is a bad one stitches may be required later. Very often in minor cases, however, the bitch will recover simply by licking herself without veterinary assistance. This is in any event not something that should affect the actual delivery of any further pups.

In the normal course of events the pups should arrive at intervals of no more than twenty minutes to half an hour, but there may be some extra large pups, or difficult breech deliveries which hold matters up. It has also to be admitted that some bitches are just naturally much slower than others, while some breeds are quite different from others, taking long rests of as much as a couple of hours between pups in some instances. Each bitch should be left to set the pace herself. It is usually possible to assist breech deliveries by a little judicious help, but care must be taken not to damage mother or pup, and if in any doubt it is better to allow the bitch to persevere unless she decides to give up after straining for some time.

If the bitch has been straining continuously for as much as half an hour or more without success it may be worth encouraging her to get up and move around. But if she is a maiden bitch who and has become exhausted and is showing signs of distress or exhaustion, especially if more than an hour and a half has passed without any sign of a further pup it is probably desirable to call in the vet. If a black and greenish discharge is seen at any time and no pup is forthcoming it means a placenta has separated and a pup should be on its way. If one does not appear then call in the vet. If veterinary assistance cannot be obtained within a couple of hours and the bitch is by then completely exhausted it may be necessary to have a Caesarean.

Although this is naturally a last resort it does not mean that all is lost by any means. It may be that the particular pup which has been holding matters up cannot be saved, but if the operation is performed in time it is possible that it may survive, and in any event the rest of the litter may well be perfectly all right. Once the wound has been stitched up it should be perfectly possible for the bitch to nurse her remaining pups successfully without any problems. Although the stitches may prove a minor complication in the short term and will have to be removed in a matter of ten days or so they should not interfere in any way with the bitch feeding the pups and there is every likelihood that she will be able to have a further litter or litters with no side effects from the operation whatsoever.

I have found myself inadvertently acting as supernumerary veterinary assistant and anaesthetist in the small hours of the morning when having had to call in the vet for a particularly stubborn birth. The results, however, on that occasion were satisfactory in that although we lost the extremely large dog pup which had been causing the problem in the first place, we managed to save the rest, and the mother, once stitched up, recovered quickly and nursed the litter successfully. That time we were lucky, but be warned that not every whelping is as fortunate. There can be occasions when everything that can go wrong appears to go wrong, but fortunately such occasions are very rare indeed.

It cannot be repeated too often that the vast majority of whelpings are perfectly straightforward with few, if any, problems which cannot be solved on the spot with a little common sense. If you are prepared for the worst the normal whelping procedure taking place as Nature intended comes as simplicity itself. Preparing everything in advance and being ready for the worst should it happen more or less ensures that the normal whelping goes with barely a hitch of any sort. At least if you know what might happen and are prepared for it if necessary the normal whelping will usually prove perfectly simple and easy and you may wonder what all the fuss was about. It is only if you are not ready and prepared for events that they are likely to turn out badly. Making proper preparations in advance should ensure a trouble free whelping for you and, more importantly, for your bitch and her pups. If you do happen to run into snags you will at least be ready for them and have some idea in advance of how to deal with them.

The time of day when the bitch decides to whelp is in the lap of the gods. In the nature of things it is usually fairly late in the evening and it will then probably continue into the early hours of the morning. This is, of course, not a hard and fast rule. It is, however, a fact that whelpings do seem to happen in the middle of the night as a general rule, most probably because this is the usual instinct in the wild and Nature is following the age-old ingrained atavistic instinct.

Fortunately, it is not always the case and the most recent whelping we had with a maiden bitch started at the very civilised hour of seven in the evening and was all over with no complications and eight healthy puppies, four of each sex, by nine the same evening. It does not often happen quite so simply or so satisfactorily, but there is no real reason why it should be very much longer unless there are complications of one sort or another, although as noted some breeds are much slower than others.

Along with the last pup there should be a final discharge of afterbirth, which the mother should at once eat if you are allowing her to do so. There is one school of thought that argues that eating afterbirth is good for the bitch and perfectly natural. Others maintain it is not good for the bitch and causes diarrhoea. Either way, it is desirable to check that the afterbirth arrives with each pup and is duly removed by you or eaten by the bitch. If it does not appear it may remain inside the bitch and either cause an unpleasant messy discharge in due course or an infection may very easily set in.

When the final pup seems to have appeared the business of tidying up the bed, as well as cleaning up the mother and checking over both her and the pups may start, while introducing them to each other and settling them in together. If there are any signs of discharge from the vagina after the birth or the bitch shows signs of discomfort and is, for instance, constantly licking herself it is advisable to check with the vet. It may be, for instance, that the delivery of a particularly large pup has overstretched and torn the vagina or vulva and the bitch needs some stitches or similar aftercare. It may, on the other hand, be that some of the afterbirth has been retained and there is the possibility an infection may result.

It is, in any event, probably desirable to have the vet in to inspect the mother and pups if you are at all worried about anything. Do not forget, however, that the costs of veterinary consultations and any medications prescribed must be deducted from the price obtained for the pups. The overall cost of breeding and rearing puppies can be sizeable as it is, without unnecessary vet's bills. You will in any event, however, want to have the vet in within a day or so at the outside if you are going to have the dew claws removed or the tails docked and unless you feel the bitch needs urgent attention at once it may be reasonable to wait until then for an overall check on the bitch and the pups. On the other hand the health of the bitch should always be paramount and if she is suffering any obvious discomfort she is unlikely to give the pups the care and attention they will require. In that case it would certainly be a false economy to delay calling in the vet.

It is always foolish in the extreme to avoid calling in a vet just to save possible costs if you are genuinely concerned about the bitch. If she appears to be in trouble and you feel it is advisable to have skilled assistance then call for help. To lose the bitch and possibly the litter at this stage to save a vet's bill, whether large or small, would be shortsighted in the extreme, to put it mildly. The bitch should always come first and her health and that of the pups should naturally be the first priority for the breeder regardless of the expense.

Breeding can be a very expensive business at times and there is no getting away from that fact. The best way to avoid unnecessary expense is to be prepared, as far as possible, for every eventuality in advance. If the bitch has been properly cared for, fed and exercised up to the birth the whelping should normally be quite straightforward and go perfectly smoothly and according to plan. As indicated there may be minor hitches here and there, but once again it cannot be emphasised too often that the vast majority of whelpings go perfectly smoothly without any major problems arising. Matters can indeed usually be left entirely to the bitch with the whelping assistant only helping out where necessary.

Assuming that this has been the case and that the whelping has gone without any particular problems, when you feel reasonably certain that the bitch has finally finished giving birth it is then desirable to check the mother over to ensure as far as possible that the last pup has finally arrived and that no more remain. Even when you have done so, although everything appears to be over and the mother has settled down happily with the pups, it is very often the way that a 'tail-end-charlie' appears unexpectedly some time later.

On more than one occasion I have returned in the morning after settling the mother down with her litter, with what I was sure was the final pup, only to find that yet another has appeared in the interval and is happily suckling along with the rest. I have even known this happen after having had to call in the vet for a particularly stubborn presentation when both he and I had thought the whelping was over with every pup finally present and accounted for and with no more to come. So even the professionals can be easily enough misled on this issue. It is perhaps a salutary lesson that most bitches can manage affairs perfectly well on their own without any assistance whatsoever from their well meaning owners.

After you are reasonably sure that the final pup has been delivered, however, and they have all been checked over to make sure of their sex and for any obvious defects, it is then time to clear up. One final check at this stage will do no harm. The remains of the umbilical cords should all be looked at once more, anointed with iodine or disinfectant again if necessary and the stomach of the pup checked over to make sure there are no obvious ruptures, which can easily enough arise. The jaws, nostrils, feet, toes and bodies should also be examined and any possible defects noted. A check for signs of any bleeding or blood pustules anywhere on the pups is important at this stage as this may well signal possible infection and if anything of this nature is discovered the vet should be informed at once.

If there is anything seriously wrong with a pup such as being born with a major deformity, a severe open rupture, or some similar major defect, it should have been noted already. It is by far the most humane thing to put it down at once as humanely as possible. Immediately at birth or at this very early stage it can be killed very simply and humanely in a number of ways. Dislocating the neck, or crushing the skull, are two methods, both instantaneous and a good deal less traumatic than drowning, which is often recommended. Frankly I do not like drowning as a means of killing any animal as it seems to take for ever and the poor beast can be seen to be struggling for what seems an age. If a vet is present it can be left to them to deal with the matter painlessly A whiff of choloroform is another effective and instantaneous method often used by vets but is not always easily available.

It is doing neither the bitch nor the pup itself any favours leaving a severely deformed, extremely sickly or damaged pup in the litter along with its healthier siblings because it will almost certainly be overlain anyway, or die a lingering death. Attempting to hand rear it separately will almost certainly be a long and painful process probably ending in failure, but at best producing a crippled or handicapped animal. The novice breeder faced with, for instance, a severely ruptured puppy, with its liver or intestines fully exposed, or some such fortunately rare condition, will almost certainly have called in the vet anyway so the final decision as to what to do can be safely left to him. He or she will have a merciful lethal injection available for just such an emergency. The owners of the bitch should, however, always be prepared to deal with matters themselves if it comes to the pinch.

If there is an obvious 'crit', i.e. a very diminutive undersized pup, which is nothing like the equal of the rest of the litter in size and strength the probability is that it will be overlain by its larger siblings if it is not overlain by the dam. It is open to question whether it is advisable in such cases to 'knock it on the head' or leave it to take its chances. Many breeders will prefer to dispose of it straight away on the principle that it will probably die anyway and that it is better to keep an even litter of healthy pups than spoil the look of it by keeping an undersized pup.

As already noted, however, where there have been several couplings during the mating there may be several pups distinctly smaller than the rest, which are in effect as much as four days younger. These will probably catch up to a large extent with their larger siblings in due course. Careful feeding and regular weighing during the next month or so should bring them on quickly enough. Pups such as these are not to be confused with a single undersized and weakly 'crit', which is usually unable to hold its own with its stronger brothers and sisters.

It is usually sensible to harden one's heart and remove any such pups at once as they will probably die later anyway, but to my mind a great deal must depend on the pup itself. I have known small pups with great character and determination which have survived and grown up to be sound specimens well able to hold their own after having had to fight determinedly from the very start. On the other hand it has to be admitted that in the majority of cases a sickly, weak and undersized pup is probably better disposed of at once because it is unlikely to live. If it is going to require special nursing, even if it does survive as a result, it is almost certainly not going to grow into a worthwhile specimen and is unlikely to be worth the effort and expense or turn out to be any sort of advertisement for your breeding. In such a case it is better to cut your losses at the start.

Being tender hearted in such circumstances is almost certainly doing the pup itself no favours and it will probably end up badly one way or another as well as undoubtedly costing extra in vet's bills, not counting all the extra time and care necessarily spent on it. Not only that, it is almost certain that you will have difficulty in selling it and may end up having to give it away unless you are prepared to be saddled with a handicapped dog. The sensible attitude is not, however, one that will appeal to everyone.

As attitudes of different people may differ widely in matters of dog training, so people may also vary widely in their attitudes to life and death. There is a tendency amongst some would-be humanitarians to try to keep alive animals which are suffering and would undoubtedly be better dead, or, to use the usual euphemism, 'put to sleep'. That less than couth old gundog trainer quoted earlier had a somewhat crude account of country life, which put the matter in perspective from the viewpoint of those who see animals born and dying frequently and to whom life and death are simple matters of everyday fact.

'There were this auld widow woman in village had an Alsatian she kept chained in yard, and it had bitten the postman and the policeman had sent word for me to come and deal with it. It had happened before because she didn't feed 'em right, only on white bread and scraps. Anyway I got a message calling me down and I knew what to expect as I'd done it before. So I were already putting gun together as I entered yard. There was postman with bandage on his hand talking to policeman and both of them looking at dog standing in the garden behind the house slavering at jaws and baying fit to bust.

' "Oh, thank you for coming so soon," says the old lady, meeting me at door. "There is just one thing I'd like to ask you. I would be so grateful if you would take collar off dog as I might need it in case I get another one. But do be careful you don't get bitten mind."

' "That's all right, Missus," I says and walks on into yard.

' "How're you going to get collar off without getting bitten?" asks policeman, looking at dog standing baying and slavering away on hindlegs at end of chain.

' "That's easy," I says, slipping a cartridge into gun and I aims at dog's chest and pulls trigger.

'We weren't long burying him and I took off collar and carried it up garden to the old widow woman.

' "Oh," she says. "You were quick. You'd hardly been gone a minute when I hears shot. I hope you had no trouble getting collar off."

' "No Missus," I says. "He were very quiet when I took collar off." '

There is no escaping the fact that even if the whelping has gone perfectly, or at least without any major problems, and there are no life or death decisions to be made, there is still almost certainly bound to be a fairly bloody and messy aftermath to clear up. After the birth of the last pup a final clean up of all the debris left behind is desirable, although the removal of the stained and soiled towels or bedding should have taken place as far as possible at the time they were being used. There will almost certainly, however, still be some to remove and replace with fresh clean bedding for the bitch and puppies before they can be left with a clear conscience. This is usually a fairly messy final clean up but it is not something that should be left to the next morning. It is definitely a task which should be finished before the bitch is finally left with her pups.

Just what type of bedding is preferred is up to each individual's choice. Rough towelling, which can be readily replaced, or similar easily washable floor covering that can be kept stretched in place and not allowed to curl up is preferable to my mind at this stage. Some people prefer newspaper, which can be replaced when wet, either laid out flat or cut or shredded. The main thing at this stage is to be able to replace it easily when it is wet, as it soon will be, and the desirable property is for it to provide warmth and purchase for the pups' feet. Underneath it all it is as well to have some completely waterproof material in place.

Later on, when the pups are older, woodshavings are some people's preferred choice. If these come from a reputable source they can be quite good. If they come from a sawmill and there is any danger of them including any possibly harmful impurities such as nails, or too much fine sawdust, which gets into the pups' eyes and mouths, it is definitely not desirable. Straw is subject to similar objections as barley straw may have prickly ends that may be troublesome to puppies, working into their skin or

Dam in whelping basket with crushed paper but no creep (Sue Rothwell) ————

Dam in whelping basket with towelling but again no creep (Sue Rothwell) ————

throats, although wheat straw does not have this drawback. Neither type of straw is good, in fact both are thoroughly undesirable, if they are old and either dusty or mouldy, although both, if fresh and clean, are often used as bedding when the pups are older and moving about freely. Shredded paper may have impurities in it such as inks and even metal clips, but again is favoured by some. Yet another type of bedding, which again has its advocates, is shredded cardboard, which is recommended as warm, absorbent and free from dust. The question of which type of bedding to use has to be a matter of personal choice as they almost all have their advantages and disadvantages. Much will probably depend on which is most readily available in your area.

Once the whelping is over and the bitch and pups have settled down, the bitch should be offered a drink of warm milk before being offered more solid food, but it should still be milky or something sloppy and easily digested. Thereafter the bitch should be offered warm and easily digested meals at regular intervals and she should, of course, have a bowl of fresh water constantly available. It is unlikely that she will want to leave the pups for any length of time at this stage, but she should be quite pleased to have the attention of her owner and some congratulatory comments on her performance, whether justified or not.

When she has finally settled down with her pups it is important to ensure that all the teats are producing milk freely and there is no hardness or swelling anywhere that might be indicative of incipient mastitis. This is always something to be on the lookout for while the bitch is nursing the pups and, for that matter, as long as she is in milk. Apart from being painful for the bitch it means that a pup on a teat affected in this way is unlikely to receive any milk. At the same time it is desirable to check once again that each pup is suckling happily and is able to hold onto the teat firmly. A weakly puppy will sometimes start to suck but then start slipping off the teat and not gaining any real benefit from its efforts to obtain a feed. It is important, therefore, to check each pup individually in turn to make sure it is getting its share of milk.

Failure to suck is one of the symptoms of fading puppy syndrome and it is not something anyone would wish to witness more than once. Fortunately this disease is no longer considered to be a threat in most areas of the UK. The effects are somewhat similar to those of herpes, which fortunately is also now very uncommon in the UK. Initially the pups begin to suck and seem to be doing quite well. Then inexplicably they just seem to fail. By degrees they start to lose the ability to suck and slowly begin to weaken, and eventually may die even if veterinary assistance is called in at once. It is a particularly distressing disease to watch as a whole litter may slowly succumb after seeming at first in fine health. It was at one time quite common and is still not unknown. Fortunately it is possible to vaccinate against this soon after the mating and it is worth checking on this with your vet. It is not expensive and is an option to consider.

In the case of pups with a herpes virus infection, the temperature of the pups drops abruptly and they may begin to show bloody pustules on the skin before dying. Keeping them warm may help, but the prognosis is poor. A vet should be called at once if what had seemed a healthy pup dies for no apparent reason or if either of these diseases is suspected.

As already indicated, keeping the pups warm from the moment they are born is a priority with a newly born litter. They should never be allowed to get cold, hence the importance of preventing draughts with a high sided whelping box and warm bedding. If necessary a covering for the box, or a heat lamp in the whelping kennel to keep the temperature constant, is strongly advised.

It should be easy to identify a well fed and contented mother and litter of young pups. They should be either suckling altogether contentedly or lying peacefully in a more or less quiescent well-fed heap with an occasional venturesome pup heading for the teats. The mother should be curled round them. The only sounds should be contented snuffling and grunts with an occasional whimper. The urine should be a clear yellow and the faeces should be a healthy yellow also. If there are any greenish or bloody movements or discoloured urine call your vet. One of the advantages of an easily replaced but tightly stretched white fluffy towel or similar base to the bed is that the remains of the urine and faeces are easy to see even when the mother is cleaning them up regularly, as she normally will.

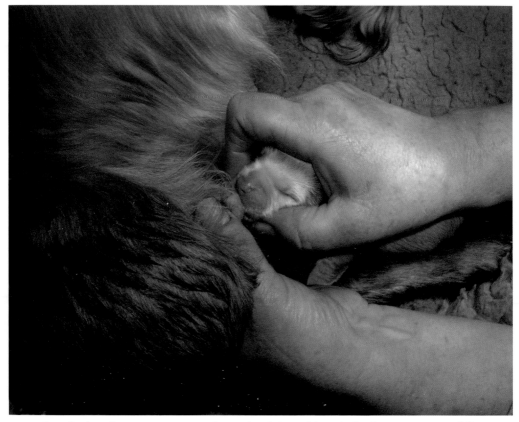

Introducing the pup to a teat and ensuring it is sucking vital colosterum successfully
(Jackie Gibbs)

A litter which is too warm will be lying in little separate heaps and may be seen to be panting a little. The mother may be lying stretched out fully and also possibly panting. Alternatively, a litter which is not warm enough will be huddled in a heap close to the mother, probably whimpering or making plaintive noises. Too active a litter at this stage is either not receiving enough food or may be not quite warm enough, or both.

Assuming all is well, however, your newly arrived litter and their mother may safely be left to their own devices once you are convinced the last pup has been born and they have all settled down with their mother. If you have a microphone installed you should be able to hear contented noises from mother and pups as well as occasional plaintive little mewing sounds as a pup is looking for a teat, with sometimes a loud shriek as the mother stirs

Pups settling with dam and suckling well but adventurous pup could be in danger of being overlaid (Jackie Gibbs)

and inadvertently puts some weight on one of the pups. If this should continue for any length of time it is advisable to investigate as a pup may well have got itself lodged behind its mother and be in danger of suffocating.

Nowadays, of course, as already pointed out, it is quite cheap to install closed-circuit TV cameras, and it may be that this is the preferred option. It is certainly better than just a microphone and saves having to look through a window at the mother and pups, or worse still disturbing her with a personal visit. If you do not have such refinements as CCTV cameras or microphone, or even a window through which to look at the pups without disturbing the dam, it is probably desirable to visit the mother and pups at hourly intervals if possible for the first couple of days. There is no need to disturb either mother or pups unduly during these visits and a quick glance should confirm that both mother and pups are doing well and that none are in danger of being overlain.

It may be an old fashioned concept but the more contact the mother has with you and the more you see of the pups the better it probably is for all concerned. There is no need to handle the pups more than necessary or disturb the bitch unduly, but accustoming the pups to the sound of a human voice and talking gently to the dam can do absolutely no harm and probably does quite a lot of good. The chance to study the pups and their so far untouched personalities at this early stage is also well worth taking. At this stage all one can really ensure is that each is suckling successfully and appears able to pass urine and defecate quite happily and without any effort, but this, in itself, is important. Apart from that, regular weighing is also important to ensure that each pup is putting on weight at much the same rate. Until the pups' eyes begin to open this should be routine and may be continued after that if it is felt necessary in any special cases.

Having delivered each pup individually it is remarkable how much may have been unconsciously learned about them already. The pup that comes into the world determined to prove itself cock of the walk can be seen shoving its siblings from the teats as soon as it is introduced to them. The noisy pups, the aggressive ones, the bullies, the determined ones, the weaklings and so on, all start to show their own particular tendencies from a very early age, indeed from the actual moment they are born in many cases.

It is in fact surprising how much can be learned from a pup's behaviour at this very early stage and personalities which are clearly developed only much later are sometimes very obvious even at this very early stage in their development. It is remarkable how, though the pups are blind and comparatively helpless, their personalities still show through. Anyway, let us face it, even newborn pups can be great fun to watch.

Once the bitch has whelped successfully and has been finally settled down with her pups, although, as suggested, the owner/handler may visit her frequently it is not desirable for too many visitors to be allowed to inspect the pups. Some bitches indeed will be very protective of their pups and may even snarl and show their teeth at their owner. Anyway, whatever their reactions, it is desirable to let them have as much peace and quiet as possible in the first week or so before the pups' eyes begin to open. The fewer outside visitors and less disturbance at this stage the better. It is definitely not advisable to let in a stream of visitors – quite apart from unsettling the bitch and disturbing the pups it is always opening up the possibility of infection of some kind, which is highly undesirable. Allowing children to handle the pups is definitely not a good idea at this stage, however well behaved they may be.

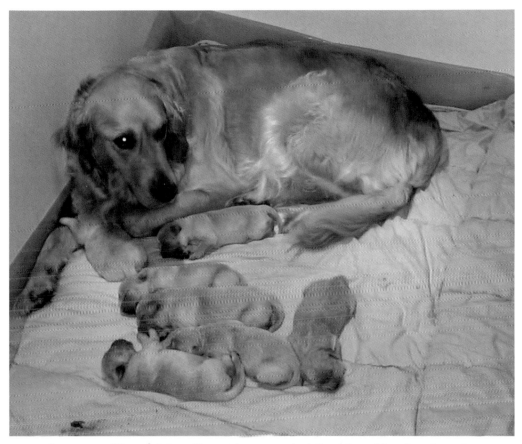

A very even litter of eight golden retriever pups just three days old under a lamp in a spacious whelping pen provided by their sheep farming owner.

It is difficult to say beforehand how the bitch will react, but if she is a little short-tempered at the best of times it is usually the case that she will be a very protective mother. I knew a Chihuahua which was always inclined to be an explosive little bitch even when by herself. She was duly mated and whelped successfully, producing one small pup not much larger than my thumb. She was fiercely protective of this tiny unattractive pink morsel of virtually naked flesh, and anyone, including her owner, putting a hand near her would find her fastened on to a finger and drawing blood. A larger sized bitch such as a lurcher or one of the gundogs may be a significant problem if not handled with care.

Even normally peaceful and quiet dogs, such as spaniels, never known to growl at anyone, may be transformed by motherhood into frighteningly

Pups in sawdust covered pen (Jackie Drakeford)

fierce and protective mothers snarling fiercely at all comers in defence of their young. So do not be surprised if this reaction is encountered in the dam to begin with. In due course she will usually settle down, although it may take a few days. If she were not a nursing mother half an aspirin in milk or similar mild sedative would will probably do no harm, but do not forget that whatever you feed the bitch is liable to be passed on to the pups in her milk. In most cases this reaction will in any event soon pass. It is best just to ignore it as far as possible.

Chapter 7 | AFTERCARE OF BITCH AND PUPS

The amount of surveillance of the dam and pups that the breeder cares to put in is entirely up to them. Some are quite content to leave it to Nature to take its course from start to finish and do not care if one or two pups are overlaid or damaged, merely putting that down to natural wastage and the survival of the fittest. This laissez-faire attitude is not, however, something any reputable breeder should accept. Unfortunately it frequently is the fittest and most venturesome pups that suffer as they crawl round behind the mother and become stuck as she moves, and then slowly suffocate. It should be the aim of any breeder with the interests of the bitch and the pups in mind to take what steps they can to prevent the loss of any of the pups once they have been whelped successfully

The methods of preventing this have already been discussed. The use of a creep to allow the pups shelter precisely in this event is all very well, but does not always work as intended. The use of a CCTV camera or microphone usually gives plenty of warning of a pup in trouble, but relies on someone being at the other end to hear it and sometimes, unavoidably, this is not the case. Constant surveillance is virtually impossible but over the first two or three days a regular hourly watch may be arranged.

If a window on the whelping kennel is available someone can usually check at regular intervals on the well being of pups and dam without disturbing them, or the bitch even being aware that she is being observed. CCTV cameras, of course, as indicated make it possible to arrange regular checks again without even going near the pups or dam. Microphones allow sound surveillance, if no more. While there are those who oppose regular visits and believe in a 'come what may' attitude, to leave it all to Nature in this way is clearly asking for trouble. Conversely, I have known people set up a camp bed for the first day or two and remain in more or less constant attendance, but this, to my mind, is overdoing things. Modern technology has now come to the rescue and made this unnecessary. One may as well take advantage of any help that is available.

There are, of course, other matters than the danger of a pup being overlaid to look out for. The old problem of fading puppy syndrome, which has been mentioned, is something that still may occur if the dam was not vaccinated against it. It is a distressing thing to watch as one pup after another, at first seemingly fit and sucking well, gradually ceases to suck and weakens visibly before finally dying. Failure to suck is one of the things that can also happen for other reasons and is always something to be on the watch for. It is not always easily noted unless care is taken to inspect each pup's reactions to being removed from the teat while it is sucking. If it does not re-attach itself fairly promptly it may have had about as much as it could manage, but it may just be failing to suck effectively. The pup which fails to suck vigorously should be examined carefully as there may be physical reasons for this such as a cleft palate, overshot or undershot jaw, or a damaged throat, or internal weakness. If in any doubt it is advisable to call in the vet as in some cases there may be internal damage and in the last resort the pup may need putting down.

The pups will, in any event, probably need their dew claws removed and if they are a working breed in which the tail is docked for other than show purposes, e.g. if a full-length tail is liable to bleed when working and develop sores, then it should also be docked. In practice both docking and removing dew claws can be performed perfectly easily the first day or at most second day after birth with a pair of sharp scissors and a cauterising machine or a dab of iodine. The first day is preferable as the sooner it is done the quicker the pups will recover. There are those who argue that this operation is unnecessarily painful and that docking the tail serves no purpose. If they have ever seen an undocked tail bleeding after waving around in gorse or even a field of thistles and seen the effect on the adult dog they would not hesitate to dock. For a pup of a day or two old the pain is negligible, eliciting nothing more than an indignant yelp. In a mature dog it is a major operation, and once the tail has developed sores it is a most unpleasant sight and will bleed every time the dog works in cover or even in a grass field.

Dew claws are found in some breeds on forelegs and hindlegs and are vestigial toes a little way up the inside of the leg. In many cases they are only found on the forelegs. In either case they are probably better removed at this stage in a working dog's life, as later on they may catch in cover or on some obstruction and if they tear away this can cause quite a serious injury in a growing or adult dog, resulting in an expensive and painful operation to remove the digit. In keeping with the modern 'humane liberal' way of thinking some vets nowadays maintain that even at this stage the pups feel considerable pain and accordingly object to removing dew claws. This strikes me as an absurd argument which cannot be substantiated.

Considering how much more pain a dog suffers if the dew claws are left on and have to be removed when they are mature this argument seems to me simply nonsense. The same is undoubtedly true for tail docking if the dog is working regularly in thick cover and suffers as a result.

At this stage the pup will barely react to the snip of the scissors and there will be only a few spots of blood, which can be stopped at once with a dab of an antiseptic such as iodine or by cauterising. Care should be taken that each pup is taken in turn and that each paw is dealt with, as, especially with a large litter, it is quite possible to overlook a pup or miss one paw. The best way of ensuring that no pup is overlooked is to have a container into which the pups that have been dealt with can be placed. To make doubly sure they should each be checked again as they are returned to their run.

Leaving even a single dew claw can be a dangerous omission. I have known a puppy whose dew claw had been accidentally left on scratch its face severely when stung by a bee and develop appalling reactions. When dealing with a litter of pups it is therefore important to make sure each pup is dealt with thoroughly in turn. While your vet is performing this task it is as well that he or she should at the same time also go and check each pup over individually to ensure that there are no problems that have been overlooked such as lesions or ruptures around the umbilical cord.

Dogs of breeds such as spaniels or pointer–retrievers where it is recommended that working dogs have their tails docked should have this done at the same time as the dew claws are removed, i.e on the second day at latest. It is a simple quick snip with the scissors and a drop of iodine, or cauterising. A slight grunt or yelp, more of indignation and surprise than of pain, is likely to be the only reaction. Anyone who has seen a long tail covered in half healed sores and bleeding in an adult undocked specimen, after working in briars or thorny cover will approve of tail docking wholeheartedly. An unprotected hairless tail waving eagerly in a field of thistles can soon become a bloody mess of sores, and the scabs formed when healing are quickly knocked off the next time the dog works. Docking in an adult is a major operation, and like removing the dew claws, may become inevitable if the dog is to work effectively and without pain. For an adult dog removing a dew claw torn on a rocky surface or a tail constantly bleeding and torn in thick cover is a tiresome, expensive and painful operation. Both can easily be dealt with as a pup at this stage.

As I write, there are moves to make docking illegal, but I trust that our legislators will leave the door open for exceptions in the case of genuine working dogs. Anyone who has seen a working dog streaming blood from a long waving tail after working hard through thorns, gorse or brambles would agree. (*See* also Appendix on page 151.)

Removing dew claws or docking tails in working dogs is not simply a cruel and unnecessary operation comparable with ear cropping and just for appearance's sake. Both of these, at this stage comparatively minor, operations are something that is better for the pup if it is to work safely in adult life without the danger of having to have a painful and expensive operation at a later date. The would-be humane liberal view of the vet who is not involved with working dogs may well be that it is unnecessary and cruel. They naturally also have the vast majority of owners of non-working dogs on their side, simply because most of them have never seen the damage that can easily result from not dealing with dew claws or tails as soon as possible. Nowadays non-working dogs and their owners are undoubtedly in the majority, but this does not mean that those owners who have working dogs and wish to protect them from pain are in the wrong. After a few years of having to dock tails of mature working dogs because they are bleeding in cover veterinary opinion is likely to change.

At this stage, of course, the pups have still not opened their eyes and they remain sightless for the first week or ten days. It is better that at this stage they are not exposed to direct sunlight or bright artificial light, and they are best kept indoors at a reasonably warm and even temperature. During this period, naturally, not only are their movements fairly circumscribed, but it is highly desirable that they should be kept within a fairly close radius of the dam in a whelping kennel or basket. They are extremely reliant on the dam and she will probably be very protective of them. The fewer strangers who see them during this period and the more privacy the dam has with them the better for all concerned.

The dam is best left alone with them and fed regularly as well as having a regular supply of fresh water available. Her food should still have vitamins added and she will need plenty to keep the supply of milk flowing freely. She may also start regurgitating feed for the pups even at this early stage. This is something which is not often seen as bitches tend to do it in private with no-one watching them. In the wild, of course, it is the natural method for the bitch to go hunting and return to the den and regurgitate her kill to provide extra feeding for the pups. The bitch herself will eat the regurgitated meal, encouraging the pups to do so as well, and there will be virtually no trace of the process a few minutes after it has taken place. Indeed some owners have never seen it and are completely unaware that it has happened.

There are, unfortunately, of course those occasions when the bitch for some reason cannot produce milk for her pups. There may be too many pups, she may have too little milk, too few teats for the number of pups, or, in the worst case scenario, she may have died or possibly picked up some

Greyhound dam still giving milk, but obviously not for much longer and a good instance of the stage when relief from pups is necessary (Jackie Drakeford)

infection and be too sick or off colour to feed the pups herself. The pups then either have to be reared by hand, which is a full time occupation, or a foster mother has to be found. This is not something easily found in a hurry and, as already noted, it is something to bear in mind as the time for the whelping approaches. If you do know of a bitch in milk before the litter is born it is always worth making sure she will be available if called on in case she is required as an emergency feeder.

Pup being hand reared with artificial milk in bottle with teat (Sue Rothwell)

If no bitch in milk is readily available, as is probably the case, there is no alternative to rearing the pups by hand. Because in such circumstances a vet will certainly have had to be called to the scene his or her help and advice will at least be available. Rearing the pups by hand is, however, an extremely time consuming operation. The milk has to be made using special milk powder and prepared at the right temperature then fed to the pups via teats attached to a special feeding bottle, which may have six or eight rubber teats. These can be obtained from most vets, chemists, or pet shops. The pups can, of course, be fed individually, but this is an even more time consuming business and with a large litter almost a round the clock occupation.

Here again the way the experienced shepherd deals with orphaned lambs can be utilised, even if the vet will have to be called on for help and advice. Artificial colosterum is obtainable and while clearly not as effective as Nature's product, is undoubtedly a great improvement on artificial milk powder, although naturally much more expensive. The experienced shepherd will warm a rubber tube and insert it carefully over the orphaned lamb's tongue, gently lowering it into the stomach. A suitable dose of the colosterum mixture can be injected direct by a syringe. After this start the orphaned lamb may then be fed artificial milk from a feeding bottle. It is vitally important however that the tube for the colosterum goes directly into the stomach and does not deviate into the lungs, as can easily happen with an inexperienced handler. That mistake will kill instantly, so if you intend to use this method of feeding it is essential to learn how to do it correctly. Careful tuition by a competent teacher is essential initially so that you know exactly what you are doing

Experienced lambers soon get used to this method of feeding colosterum, as do some regular dog breeders. It is generally too expensive to keep feeding colosterum to lambs, but can be justified in the case of a motherless litter of pups. Despite the added expense it has many advantages, both in beneficial results and in speed, over trying to feed a number of pups solely

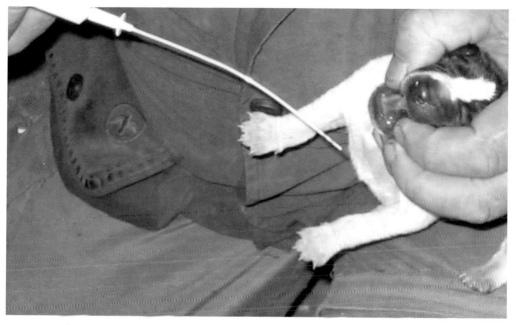

Pup about to have tube inserted direct to stomach to feed artificial puppy colosterum
(Tom Brechney)

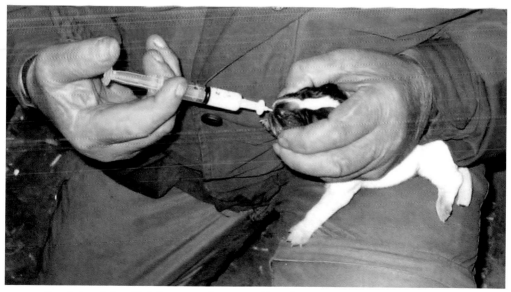

Pup being fed artificial puppy colosterum direct by tube reinforced by tom cat catheter
(Tom Brechney)

by artificial teats. It is well worth patiently taking the time to learn how to feed by this method should the unfortunate position arise where it may be necessary. Like most such matters, once learned, it seems comparatively simple. Some experienced dog breeders feed their pups supplementary colosterum in this way even where the bitch is feeding them naturally, though whether this is entirely desirable may be open to question. The novice breeder should, however, certainly not try this without first taking veterinary advice and guidance on both a suitable dosage for the pups and how to administer it correctly.

Naturally enough, the rubber tube used for feeding pups by this process is thinner than that used for lambs, and one breeder I know finds it easier to reinforce it with a very light metal tom cat's catheter, which he also obtains from his vet. Rather than warm these in water he runs them through his mouth once or twice beforehand, which supplies the warmth required. He then slips the tubes gently down the throat of his puppies before injecting the required dose of colosterum. As they grow older the pups tend to damage the catheter and he quite often has to replace it, so that one veterinary assistant actually thought he was breeding cats rather than puppies.

Without such means of fast feeding, it is, of course quite a lengthy process providing milk for a motherless litter. It involves sterilising the teats on each occasion and preparing the milk to the right temperature, and repeating the process at regular intervals through twenty-four hours, as well as ensuring that each pup has its fair ration. It has at least the merit that the breeder comes to know the pups intimately and has a very clear idea of the temperament and strength of each individual pup before they have even opened their eyes. It is surprising how much of the character of the future animal can be revealed at this early stage when the breeder is intimately connected with them for lengthy periods. The determined pup, the lazy pup, as well as the strong and the weakly, the noisy and the quiet, all are traits quickly distinguished. From an early age the intelligent, the stupid, the greedy, the bully and the readily cowed are easily recognised. To a large extent these traits will remain the same in adult life.

During this early stage, especially when feeding by hand an essential piece of equipment is an accurate weighing machine. This can be either a set of mechanical scales, such as are used in most kitchens, which is probably best and most convenient, or a simple spring balance. The former is probably easiest as the pups can be laid on a light padded bed and the weight is shown on a large dial. A simple spring balance is also quite effective, but the pup has to be held in a sling beneath it and the dial is usually much smaller. A piece of thick bandage secured with Velcro or a

The bitch regurgitates to the litter while they suckle. Most bitches instinctively prefer to feed their pups in this way out of sight. Some breeders never see it happening. ——

large safety pin is quite effective for holding the pups, or a small harness may be preferred because as they get older they can become somewhat wriggly. If required, a bandage secured by Velcro or a large safety pin holding the pups on the bed above the scales is really easier, but either can be quite effective. The main point is to be able to check their weight easily and regularly during the early growing period, however it is done. Regular and steady weight gain is essential.

Ideally the pups should be examined and weighed twice daily from the moment of birth, and the results noted carefully, hence the importance of being able to distinguish the pups easily, using individual indelible numbers if necessary. Any signs of weight loss are very much a danger signal as the weight should be increasing steadily. If the pups are not gaining weight and the dam seems short of milk they may need to be fed special supplementary milk, i.e. reconstituted powdered milk, or colosterum, by hand. Should weight loss persist then call the vet at once.

If any pup at this stage shows signs of looking poorly it is always advisable to take its temperature by inserting a thermometer into its rectum. The temperature should be 97–102°F (roughly 36–39°C) and anything less than this is a cause for concern. In the early stages it is very important to ensure that the pups are kept warm, and their temperatures should always be between 97 and 102°F. Anything over 102°F (39°C) and they may be running a fever. If the temperature is too high or too low, call the vet.

The pups' stools and urine should also be checked daily for any signs of blood or discolouration. Any such signs, again, are a danger signal and in either case the vet should at least be informed. After the first ten days or so the dangers from killer infections such as herpes and fading puppy syndrome are more or less past, but care should still be exercised.

From the time of birth for the next few weeks there is one point that should be watched out for, especially with a maiden bitch nursing a large number of pups. If the bitch is seen to be walking stiffly round and looking anxious, then lying down and trembling, and not paying the usual attention to the pups, these are all typical signs of milk fever, or eclampsia, which is potentially fatal. It is, however, easily cured by an injection of calcium. While not something to be unduly anxious about, it is something to keep a weather eye out for and if it seems to be present call the vet and have the injection as soon as possible. Without treatment milk fever can result in the death of the bitch within quite a short time.

In a healthy thriving litter the pups should in general look fat, well fed and contented. If they are complaining and huddling up, or do not feel warm to the touch, this is a bad sign. It may, of course, just be that the whelping room, or kennel, itself is too cold and the pups are feeling chilled. If this is the case and artificial heating is not available, or has failed for some reason, the whelping box should be covered and the dam and pups will then work up a satisfactory heat, much as they would in a den in the wild.

Once the pups begin to open their eyes the most dangerous period is past and their horizons begin to develop very quickly. By this time they will begin standing on their hindlegs and scrabbling at the confines of their surroundings. It is only a matter of time before they will need to be given a larger space in which to roam, as well as somewhere to release the increasing amounts of liquid they are imbibing. Keeping their sleeping area dry will become an increasing problem and no longer one that their dam can solve by licking their backsides and their puddles.

The question of when to move them to a larger area is dependent on the circumstances. The ideal whelping kennel should be a room with a doorway giving access to a larger space, part of which could be covered and part preferably open. Once the pups start opening their eyes and need wider horizons they may be allowed access to the whole room in which their box/basket/container is situated. After a few more days, when it is judged they have matured sufficiently, have their eyes fully open and are becoming

Pups with shredded paper in pen (Jackie Drakeford)

even more venturesome, the door to the great outdoors may at last be opened. From then on their progress should be fairly rapid.

The process of the pups opening their eyes is in itself a somewhat anxious period. Usually there is no trouble. First of all one or two eyes will be seen to open and blue apparently sightless balls will be visible. Then, gradually, the whole litter hopefully will be seen to be crawling around with their eyes all more or less open. After a day or so, by which time they should all be moving around confidently, it is as well to check each one in turn and as far as possible ensure that their sight appears to be functioning normally. This is something that is worth checking again more carefully in a week or so when the pups are more developed and it is easier to check their reactions. Simply moving the hand before each eye should initially be sufficient to test the sight reaction. Later, if there are any doubts about any of them, more thorough testing may be worthwhile.

By this time the pups will be nearly at the end of their second week and they may even be introduced to milk feeding, especially if it is felt that the mother is having any trouble feeding them. This is a fairly straightforward process involving small shallow bowls with a supply of slightly warmed

Sitting at command, whistle and signal; at six to seven weeks: ready for food and soon to leave for new homes

milk and showing each pup in turn how to drink. This may involve offering a milky finger to suck from the bowl, or dunking their nose in the milk if necessary, but after initial splutters the message soon gets home and milky faces are soon part of the daily scene.

It is, incidentally, a good plan at this stage to introduce the pups to a call and whistle to bring them out to the new source of food. Such basic discipline taught at this tender age stays with them and when they show impatience it is never too early to hold the dish above them and give the command 'sit' along with a long 'drop' whistle. Because the dish is above them they will do this naturally, and it is little problem to ensure obedience even if your feet may be mobbed initially. Stick to it and you will have well behaved puppies to impress prospective purchasers simply as a result of this regular early very basic training. This initial obedience training cannot be started too early, and the earlier it starts the less trouble the pups will be as they grow older.

Individual mince meat balls at around five weeks – soon consumed

By this time the pups should all be developing distinct personalities and some obvious variations in size may be starting to show themselves. This is common enough between dogs and bitches, with the former usually having a tendency to be slightly larger and more heavily boned. The markings, too, where the litter are not all one colour, will begin to show more clearly and distinguish the pups more obviously. From this stage onwards they become increasingly interesting to watch as their differing and distinctive personalities begin to show themselves.

Once the pups have access to the outside kennelling and run, and as they become more demanding, it is also important that the dam should have somewhere she can retreat to for an occasional rest from them. A raised platform in the run or by the kennel will provide her with a refuge from them when required. During the first few weeks this may not be used, but as the pups develop needle sharp little teeth and become ever more demanding her teats are likely to become increasingly sore at times. This is when she will need to have some means of getting away from them for an occasional rest.

By the fourth or fifth week, depending on their development, the pups may be introduced for the first time to small balls of fresh raw mince. These should not be much larger than the size of a thimble to start with, but it is surprising how quickly they will take to eating them – perhaps 'devouring' them would be a better description of most puppies' first reactions to raw meat. They should initially be fed individually to make sure that each has its fair share. Only latterly, as they begin to grow sufficiently to hold their own, should they be fed communally, and, to begin with at least, care should be taken that there is no bullying and that equal shares for all prevail. In some cases it may even be necessary to continue with individual bowls for the weaker or less aggressive members of the litter in order to prevent them losing out to their stronger siblings.

By this time, almost certainly, they will have been introduced by the dam to regurgitated meals and will have already tasted something approaching solid food rather than pure liquid. From this time onwards their progress should be fairly straightforward as far as feeding goes. By the sixth week they should be onto regular meals of mince, and daily milk meals as well. These should, of course, be fed at regularly spaced intervals throughout the day, and the practice of calling the pups by voice and whistle and making them sit to the verbal command 'sit' and the drop whistle should be steadily continued to form a daily habit. If it is regularly enforced from the very beginning this is a drill to which the puppies should soon become accustomed. Once they realise that they are not fed until they have accepted this regular practice they should quickly enough obey these simple commands. There must, however, be no relaxation of this routine or they will quickly revert to a disorganised and disobedient scrum at feed times, mobbing their handler and each intent on securing as much as possible.

As soon as the pups start eating solid food it is time to consider worming them. Some of the pups may already be showing signs of distended abdomens, and even sometimes worms in their stools. Whether your vet recommends a powder in the food or liquid worming the results are much the same. The amount of worms a pup may have at this stage is surprising, but they are usually easily enough dealt with. They seldom cause any problems if they are dealt with routinely, but if in any doubt it is probably wise to check with your vet

This is the stage in the puppies' lives when they really need stuffing full of good nutritious feed. It is a false economy not to feed them well with good minced beef at this stage, and to use good quality milk. The bitch, too, will need feeding up and should also be fed well in order to keep up her

Worming pup by syringe at around four to five weeks (Jackie Gibbs)

supply of milk, although by this time her main contribution to the pup's welfare will probably be regurgitating her own meals for them. The importance of this good early start is easily seen if you can compare pups that have been well fed and those which have not been so well looked after at this critical stage. The difference will be very noticeable and the well fed pups in good condition will be very much more saleable. This is the point the breeder should appreciate. The pups may have required more feeding but they will look a credit to the kennel and the bitch and they are infinitely more saleable than the others which have not received as good a quality of care at this important stage of their lives.

While watching the pups at play and feeding the breeder should already have a very good idea of their individual characteristics and know which are the forward pups and which the retiring ones. It is important to make sure there is no bullying by the larger more forward members of the litter, and

Pups at around four weeks at communal milk dish

any tendency in this direction should be firmly checked. A close eye at feeding times should soon ensure that there is no excessive harassment of the less forward pups, although there will always be a certain amount of scrimmaging. Where necessary it is as well to divide feeding into separate bowls and ensure that all have an equal share while obeying the commands to sit and wait. Even if this takes a little longer it is time well spent because the pups will have obedience to essential commands ingrained from an early age. It is surprising how effective such early training can be, and the earlier it is started the easier it becomes to enforce, but strict enforcement is essential at all times. One lapse can seriously undermine weeks of work.

By this time, various puppy toys to keep the litter occupied may have been profitably introduced to the outside kennel. Whether these are rubber bones or large rubber balls hardly matters. The thing to do is avoid any very small toys, or easily destructible fluffy ones, which may stick in the pups' throats and cause them to choke. They will, in any event, probably make do with sticks or bits of towelling or anything they can find. It is important, however, to make sure that there is nothing harmful they can get hold of in the kennel area. Small stones or sticks may be swallowed or may get stuck and cause pups to choke. Bits of glass or old nails and similar objects such as pieces of barbed wire, which may have been lodged in a hedge root for years, should have been removed, but may have been dug up and discovered by enquiring puppies rootling in the earth of their kennel run. Even archaeologists would be surprised by what puppies can dig up!

It is always worth checking the kennel and the yard daily for any such objects, which may have suddenly appeared miraculously out of nowhere and which may result in serious injury to a pup which experiments with it. Old razor blades, broken glass, coils of wire, marbles and all sorts of odds and ends, including on one occasion a hearing aid dropped by a visitor in the grass, are amongst the numerous oddments I have found from time to time that pups have retrieved or been attempting to eat. I am no longer surprised by any oddities inexplicably turned up by puppies in areas which I had previously combed systematically and could have sworn were free of any dangerous materials and perfectly safe.

Any kennel yard that is not entirely secluded is especially prone to the sudden appearance of odds and ends. Where a wall borders an area used by other people there is always a danger of unexpected objects suddenly appearing apparently from nowhere. Bits of wire, bottles, plastic bags especially, and other rubbish can materialise out of nowhere, possibly sometimes just carried by the wind. Airborne plastic bags are a particularly tiresome problem and balloons released in various publicity extravaganzas also have a habit of arriving unexpectedly from time to time. Although in the main these are harmless, it is wise to check frequently for any such detritus which might adversely affect the pups.

Although it may sound rather unlikely another possible source of trouble, for spring litters especially, can be the appearance of wasp nests. If the kennel is outside with a grass run it is quite common in some years for wasps to start nesting in grass runs or in the kennel itself. I have known two or three ground tunnel nests appear almost overnight in a grass run and have only seen them because the grass has been cut and the wasps could be seen leaving and returning to the nest. The bitch herself is probably sensible enough to avoid being stung, although it is always a possibility, and one best avoided by getting rid of the nest at once. An inquisitive pup, however, could easily be stung in the face or nose. This is a much more common occurrence than might be thought and the consequences can be very serious, indeed life threatening, if a pup should suffer a severe reaction to the sting.

As well as wasps, bees can sometimes prove a problem when swarming in the spring and summer months, and it is always wise to keep an eye open for them and other insects that may be troublesome. Infestations of ants, midges or hordes of flies can all be a possible source of trouble if they suddenly appear in large numbers in hot weather. Keeping the kennel well disinfected is a wise consideration. With the pups out of the way, spraying regularly with Jeyes fluid is a very sensible precaution.

Four legged pests such as mice and rats may also be found from time to time, if there are any scraps of food around, and may or may not cause a problem. In some places mink can also be a factor to take into consideration. A hunting mink can easily kill a small puppy, and they are now very common in many parts of the country. A few tunnel traps set around outside the kennel yard cannot go amiss if there is any likelihood of any such pests appearing as long, of course, as there is no possibility of the pups having access to them. In some parts of the country buzzards are now so plentiful that they too may constitute a hazard as they have been known to swoop down and seize small dogs and puppies. If there is any serious danger from them, as they are protected birds and cannot be trapped or shot, netting the kennel yard or rigging up a scarecrow or a dummy hawk would seem to be the best possible means of protection.

By the sixth week the pups should all be eating mince and drinking milk, although still suckling the dam and receiving regurgitated feed from her. While probably still heavy with milk, the dam by this time is likely to be showing signs of scratches and rawness on the teats from the sharp claws and teeth of the pups. As the feed for the pups is gradually increased each day so the time the bitch spends feeding them should correspondingly be reduced. By the seventh to eighth week the pups should be fully weaned and ready to leave for their new homes.

It is desirable, therefore, on several counts that the pups should be removed as soon as possible once they are fully weaned. To be left with a kennel full of weaned puppies eating their heads off is a nightmare that no owner who has once experienced it will wish to repeat. The prospective owners should by this time all have booked their puppies, preferably in advance of the mating, and chosen them individually in the past two or three weeks as soon as the pups started on solid food. There should therefore be little problem in arranging times for their departure when they are finally weaned. Prospective owners are usually keen to have them as soon as possible, but if they wish you to keep a pup for them for any reason it is as

Pups in pen with fitted towelling

well to make sure that that you receive a down payment and agreed charges for its kennelling and keep.

It is important, however, where there are two or sometimes more puppies in a litter which are very alike, to make sure that there are no mix-ups when it comes to the pups being removed. Use of an indelible marker dye can be helpful in such cases to make sure there are no arguments when it comes to the pup being taken away. Some would-be owners can be very unsure which pup they prefer most from a litter and when it comes to taking their pup away may wish to change their minds at the last minute. It is desirable in such cases to make sure there are no mix-ups, while at the same time doing your best for both pup and prospective owner. If you have any doubts about a would-be purchaser who cannot make up their mind it may be advisable to insist on a deposit, or money upfront, when they make their decision, if they are not taking the pup immediately. A payment made then concentrates the mind wonderfully.

A novice breeder is not in the same league as a successful professional

Raised platform for bitch to escape pups' attentions ────────────

breeder who may often check any prospective purchasers' credentials and suitability very closely before making a sale. On the other hand no-one wishes to see a pup they have bred going to anything but a good home. This, unfortunately, is not always easy to ensure in advance and it is sometimes difficult to know just how good an owner some prospective purchasers are likely to be. It is probably best to try to restrict sales to people who have been recommended to you as sound homes by people on whom you can rely. If you have been advertising sufficiently widely in advance you may even find that you are in a position to pick and choose the homes for your pups. This is another reason for making sure this is a priority.

When parting with the pups it is important, of course, to ensure that all the necessary documentation is completed. The necessary Kennel Club registration papers must of course be completed and the new owner's name inserted and signature duly entered on the forms. To obtain the registration documents the signature of the owner of the sire will also be required. Choice of a kennel name for registration of the pups, if you have not already got one, may take a little while to be approved and is a further expense. If the pups have been vaccinated then again the necessary papers need to be completed and passed to the new owners. In most cases the pup will need to be tattooed, or microchipped, for permanent identification and in that case, again, the necessary papers must be included. Most of these costs should of course be borne by the buyer of the pup not by the breeder, but the paperwork involved is the breeder's responsibility and it all takes time.

The Kennel Club, although helpful and efficient, has a vast amount of correspondence to deal with and this can be a lengthy procedure, so it is as well to start applying for registration as soon as the litter is born and the sexes of the pups are known. Names should have been chosen beforehand so that the minimum of time is wasted on sending off the necessary forms. If you intend to breed again or on a regular basis it is a sound policy to choose names from the letters of the alphabet to be able to distinguish easily between the various litters at a later date.

If any pup is being sent abroad then a whole new vista opens up. Each country has its own set of instructions for injections and methods of carriage, as well as different sets of papers to be filled in, usually in triplicate. Embassies have to be approached and the necessary forms obtained and veterinary injections and inspections passed. This can be a minefield and is perhaps best be left to specialist firms, who deal with exporting dogs as a matter of course. This, however, naturally comes at a price and not all these firms are necessarily as scrupulous or efficient as their glossy brochures would have you believe. Indeed in some cases the costs can soar unbelievably high. It is wise to ensure that these costs go directly to the new owner.

The trouble with overseas sales of pups is that each country has different requirements and rules. While some are comparatively simple others are specific to a sometimes painstaking degree, requiring forms signed by Ministry officials and veterinary surgeons immediately prior to the date of departure. This can often be extremely difficult to arrange, especially at weekends. Some countries, such as New Zealand, insist on no injection against leptospirosis as the disease is kept out of the country and injected dogs might possibly introduce it. Others insist on injections against exotic diseases.

If a letter is delayed in the post, or the time limit for an injection has expired, the whole process may have to be repeated and the pup's departure delayed. Then again, if a flight is delayed for some reason beyond the owner's control, such as a strike of cabin crew or air traffic controllers, or some such comparatively common glitch, the whole process may also have to be repeated. Any such delays may mean that by the time another flight can be arranged the pup may have grown and the original container prepared for it may be too small and a new container may have to be purchased. There are innumerable comparatively minor problems which can and do arise when sending pups abroad.

Such problems can, however, be both expensive and time consuming. It is essential, therefore, to ensure before starting that all such expenses are borne by the overseas buyer otherwise it is easy to end up considerably out of pocket. Again it is important if possible to insist on seeing the dog onto the plane. You are not allowed to sedate dogs in most cases and I have known of pups being loaded onto planes as the jet engines were being tested. To be transported in a closed container behind jet engines when they were being revved up to full pitch must be a shattering ordeal. Not surprisingly the pups are likely to arrive at the other end still terrified and may remain in a highly nervous state for several weeks, if not traumatised for life. Such results, of course, while no fault of yours, will inevitably reflect on you as the breeder.

Sending dogs to the Antipodes before the era of regular flights was a comparatively simple process as they went by sea and their quarantine was counted in their time at sea, so that they usually went straight to their new owner on arrival. On the other hand they spent six weeks or more at the mercy of the crew. Admittedly this could be all right if there were dog minded crew members, when they tended to be thoroughly spoiled. On one occasion, however, despite written instructions to the contrary, a fine dog pup I had sent over was secured to the deck rail and somehow managed to leap overboard in the Red Sea. The account I was sent of what happened next was harrowing. A boat was launched as he was seen swimming after the ship but a shark got to him before the crew. I also gathered from the recipient at the other end that the feed that had been sent with them had been allowed to become contaminated with salt water and the other two animals were in very poor condition.

That was the last time I sent any dogs by that shipping line, but unfortunately the trouble with sending dogs or other animals by sea or air is simply that the animals are at the mercy of other human beings who may not be either thoughtful or experienced when it comes to handling animals. On that occasion I had provided the ship's officers with three pages of carefully worded instructions in triplicate to avoid any problems. I insisted that the first mate, who received the dogs, should read them through and see if he had any queries. After taking his time doing so, he said, 'I have only one query'. On my asking what it was he amazed me by asking: 'Which is the dog and which are the bitches ?' I should have removed them at once on the spot, but having driven to Liverpool with them I was reluctant to take such drastic action. I still regret it.

In the main it has to be said in their defence, however, that most of the staff handling animals in transport nowadays are well trained and thoughtful. It is, however, almost certainly bound to be a traumatic experience for any puppy to be suddenly removed from its accustomed comfortable surroundings and the company of its mother and siblings, its regular meals and routines, then suddenly enclosed in a darkened container, subjected to buffetings and unaccustomed terrifying sounds of jet engines nearby and strange voices and unpleasant smells. It is bound to affect even the most ebullient puppy adversely, however much care is taken during the journey. It is therefore advisable to think twice before sending a puppy abroad. The costs and the hassle are substantial and the strain on the pup is probably immense. It is really surprising how well most of them cope with the stresses involved.

Since they can mount up very considerably, the costs of transfer of a pup to the new owner, the cost of KC Registrations, of inoculations, of microchipping or tattooing the dog and any costs of transport to its new home, should, of course, as pointed out, be borne by the new owner. If the breeders were to pay these costs they would be very much out of pocket by the end of the deal because the veterinary costs of certificates and injections alone in many cases can be large. This is one more reason why it is important to have sold the pups well in advance if possible. There should then at least be less of a cash flow problem and there may even be the encouraging prospect of ending up with a small profit margin at the end of the day.

The trouble with not having sold them at this stage is that the cost of keeping the pups begins to escalate alarmingly as they grow older. Anyone who has kept puppies will know how each day it seems they are capable of consuming more and more food. Furthermore the pups themselves become more demanding, requiring individual attention, exercise, as well as initial lessons in work and obedience training, and still every day they seem to be eating more. Very quickly this all becomes not only time consuming and arduous but expensive.

Without this time consuming training, on the other hand, you will have large and uncontrollable gangly animals bouncing about and barking at everything and everyone, which are no sort of advertisement for your breeding and also very difficult to sell to anyone. The whole effect is cumulative, and the pups themselves are rapidly growing from the attractive very saleable puppy stage into the gawky rather unattractive gangly teenage stage when they are not so easily sold. This is the time when the novice breeder understandably begins to panic as the bills mount and any possible profits vanish into limbo.

The professional breeder may well decide as a matter of course to keep one or two likely puppies to train on and sell at a later date as half-trained prospects or fully trained dogs. Indeed he or she may not be greatly troubled if one or two pups remain unsold, as it is probably as easy to keep two or more to train on together as it is to keep one. The reverse, of course, tends to be the case with the amateur breeder who probably does not have the time or the space of the professional breeder and is likely to find keeping more than one puppy a serious problem.

These are not points that the amateur breeder who has decided it would be nice to breed a litter of puppies normally considers until it is too late. Only when the pups are eight weeks old or more and the expenses are mounting daily with the pups themselves growing apace does the horrid truth begin to dawn. By then it is too late, and the pups may end up being virtually given away while the would-be breeder sadly adds up his or her losses and vows never to breed again.

With a little forethought and preparation, however, anyone deciding to breed can in fact ensure that they end up with a satisfactory puppy that they have bred and may even end up in pocket to some extent into the bargain. There is never any guarantee of this, of course, but with reasonable forward planning and if they are prepared to face the fact that not everything will necessarily work out exactly as planned, indeed that there may be catastrophes along the way, then they are at least on the right lines. In general, if they are prepared to accept the rough with the smooth, they will probably find everything works out satisfactorily in the end.

Whether they will wish to repeat the performance is, of course, another matter. It does, however, undoubtedly have a fascination for those who are interested in planning ahead and seeing how the progeny of their own breeding develop over the years. This, however, means planning several years ahead and is rather like looking into a crystal ball. The results may or may not be worthwhile.

There is, however, undoubtedly a similar vicarious satisfaction to that of watching your children be successful at school, in university or in later life in seeing a litter you have bred prove successful as they develop. If they start winning in tests or trials and go on to become first rate working dogs, as well as possibly themselves sires and dams of further successful litters it is difficult not to be very pleased. To know that the bloodline you have initiated has proved a successful one is indeed very gratifying. To know that it may have had a favourable effect on a breed is bound to be a considerable satisfaction to anyone fortunate and far seeing enough to have achieved this goal. That, after all, should be the aim of the dedicated professional or experienced amateur breeder.

The first-time amateur breeder should be pleased enough if any of the litter of pups they bred does well, especially the one they chose to keep. This is usually the immediate aim of the exercise for them. If that in itself can be achieved then it should all have been worthwhile, and undoubtedly the amateur breeder will have learned a few important lessons in the process. Should he or she decide to breed again at least they will recognise those mistakes they made the first time round and try to avoid them as far as possible. They may even feel they are now in a position to advise other would-be breeders on what to expect.

The pitfalls of breeding dogs are really much the same as the pitfalls of having children. Few human beings, in fact marry or take a partner simply with a view to having children. In the same way few amateur dog owners buy a bitch puppy with an immediate viewpoint of breeding from her. The average dog owner simply buys a dog or a bitch because he or she likes the breed, or because they have known others of the same kind and think they would be pleasant to own. It is usually only as the bitch becomes older that the thought of breeding from her begins to be considered seriously.

The unthinking owner of a handsome bitch may be approached by someone who asks them if they might consider breeding from her as they would like a pup out of her, or there may be a nearby dog which catches their eye and puts the idea in their mind as they see the two of them gambolling together. They may, alternatively, just see an attractive litter of puppies and the idea of breeding follows. However the idea may arise, the effects are the same. Once the insidious thought is there the rest will almost certainly follow and the first steps on the slippery slope are taken.

It all seems so simple and natural, and in so many cases it is. There are, however, a number of points to consider along the way and it is to be hoped that this book will make at least a few of them clear. If, despite having learned some of the possible pitfalls that await the novice breeder, you are still determined to breed from your bitch and you have had the all clear from your vet that she is strong and healthy with no obvious weaknesses, then go ahead.

Choose the sire with care, make sure the mating goes well, feed and exercise the bitch well, spread the word long in advance of the expected litter, prepare everything for the pups beforehand and be ready for them when they arrive. There is every likelihood that it will all be perfectly straightforward with everything going according to plan. It only remains to wish both of you good luck and healthy pups.

Appendix | THE TAIL DOCKING OF WORKING DOGS LEGISLATION

The docking of dogs' tails has been under attack from various organised and vociferous quarters for many years. Animal activists and other more socially acceptable pressure groups have long cited this as an example, as they see it, of needless cruelty. No-one would wish to condone unnecessary surgery on dogs such as ear cropping, or indeed tail docking, simply for show purposes, but there are certain categories of working dogs that need to have their tails docked as puppies to prevent the likelihood of injury when working as an adult dog and then having to have major surgery. The working dogs, which require their tails to be docked to prevent injury when working are the groups which include spaniels, (Springers, Cockers, Clumbers, etc) the Hunt Point and Retrieve breeds (German Shorthaired Pointers, Weimaraners, Hungarian Viszlas, etc) and working terriers.

As an amateur breeder of my own bloodline and, having had German Shorthaired Pointers (GSPs) for fifty years and having usually docked my own pups, I can speak from personal experience. I have docked over ten litters averaging about eight dogs in each at a day old when they clearly feel virtually no pain. The only reaction at that early stage is likely to be a grunt or a small yelp of indignation rather than pain. It is all over in a second followed by a dab of iodine or cauterisation to avoid infection. It is, however, essential to dock within twenty-four hours of whelping or forty-eight at the latest.

Like most of the HPR breeds the GSPs are originally a cross and the undocked tail tends usually to have little or no feathering or protection being thin and easily damaged in thorny cover. I have seen an undocked dog's tail bleeding after working in thick cover. Once this happens sores develop easily and the mature dog requires its tail docked to continue working. This is a major operation in an adult dog as well as being expensive. Undocked spaniels with their long hairy curly tails waving busily when working hard in thick cover such as brambles or wild briars are also particularly prone to injury, sometimes becoming almost inextricably entangled in thorny stems and badly torn. They too then require amputation to continue working. Terriers working down rabbit or rat holes or fox's earths often have to be extricated by their tails and unless these are docked they may easily be broken in the process. There is thus a very good reason for docking in each of these cases if the dog is working regularly.

Unfortunately, as with foxhunting, the emotive passions aroused over the issue of docking dogs has triumphed over the experience of those directly concerned. The feeling that this must be cruel to the animal, supported by the views of many veterinary bodies, has overruled the views of the dog owners directly concerned represented by the Kennel Club. The veterinary view has been coloured by the fact that very few vets have ever seen a bleeding tail since almost all the working dogs concerned have been docked for the past century. Unfortunately laws have now been passed in England, Wales and Northern Ireland banning the docking of dogs unless they are to be used for shooting. If they are docked they may not be shown, thus preventing any dual champions in field trials and the show ring ever being produced again. This means that the split between show dogs and working dogs in the breeds concerned is now confirmed and will eventually result in separate types developing within these breeds, which is something that generations of breeders and the Kennel Club have tried to prevent.

Worse still the legislation is not even similar throughout the UK. The late Labour legislature Scotland has banned docking altogether under the emotive wording 'Mutilation of Dogs Act'. The current situation is bewildering to say the least and is heavily weighted against the Scots as opposed to everyone else in the UK. At present the average Scottish working dog owner of the breeds concerned has little incentive to breed if the dogs cannot be docked and sold elsewhere in the UK or abroad. Anyone inside or outside Scotland who wants a dog of these working breeds is being virtually forced to buy a docked dog from elsewhere in the UK, which is absurd. This legislation in Scotland is equivalent to shooting oneself in the foot. The only people likely to gain anything are the veterinary supporters of the ban who will find they have a gradual demand for docking working dogs with bleeding tails and will then change their minds about the advisability of docking pups since it is not a pleasant operation to have to do on a mature dog.

The sooner this Act is revised the better, if only on the lines of the legislation in England so that there is then a level playing field for all breeders of the working dogs concerned in the UK. Completely revoking it would be better and more sensible since, any further division between working and show dogs within the breeds concerned is highly undesirable. Clearly this legislation should not be left as it stands and needs revision, or completely revoking, as a matter of urgency for the sake of the animals concerned if not their owners.